SHONEN JUMP MANGA

YuYu HAKUSHO™

Vol. 11

Eat or Be Eaten!!

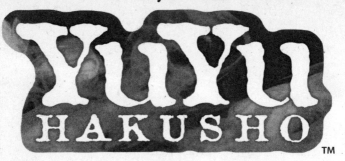

STORY AND ART BY

YOSHIHIRO TOGASHI

CAST OF CHARACTERS:
TEAM URAMESHI
KURAMA
KAZUMA KUWABARA
GENKAI
YUSUKE URAMESHI
HIEI
SHIZURU KUWABARA
ATSUKO URAMESHI
BOTAN
KEIKO YUKIMURA
YUKINA

THE DAY BEFORE THE STORM!!

THE DAY BEFORE THE STORM!!

SPROING
HAH!!!
WHAM!!

BWOOM
RRRUMBLE
BLAST...!
BY TOMOR-ROW...
...I WILL MASTER THE BLACK DRAGON!!

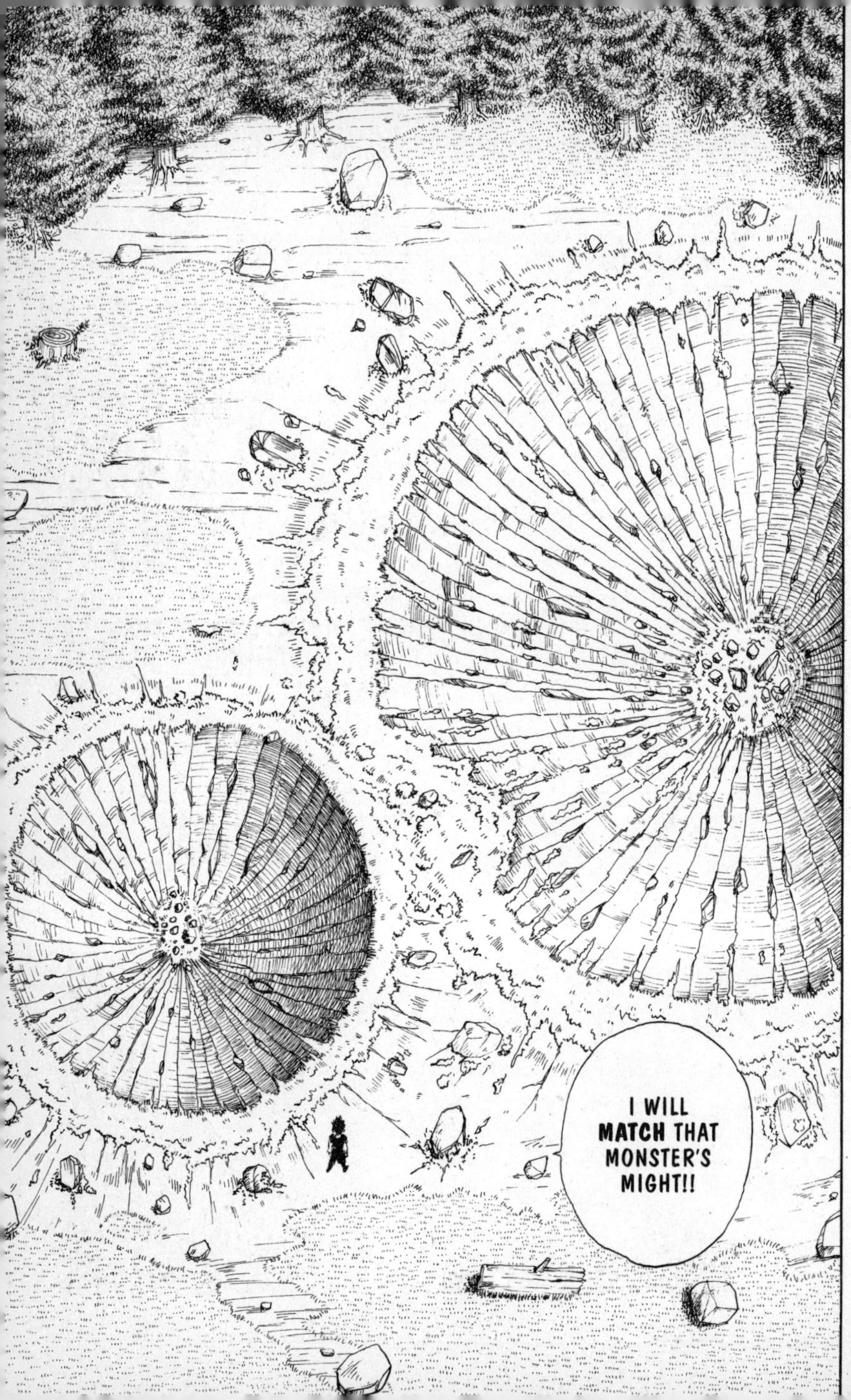
I WILL MATCH THAT MONSTER'S MIGHT!!

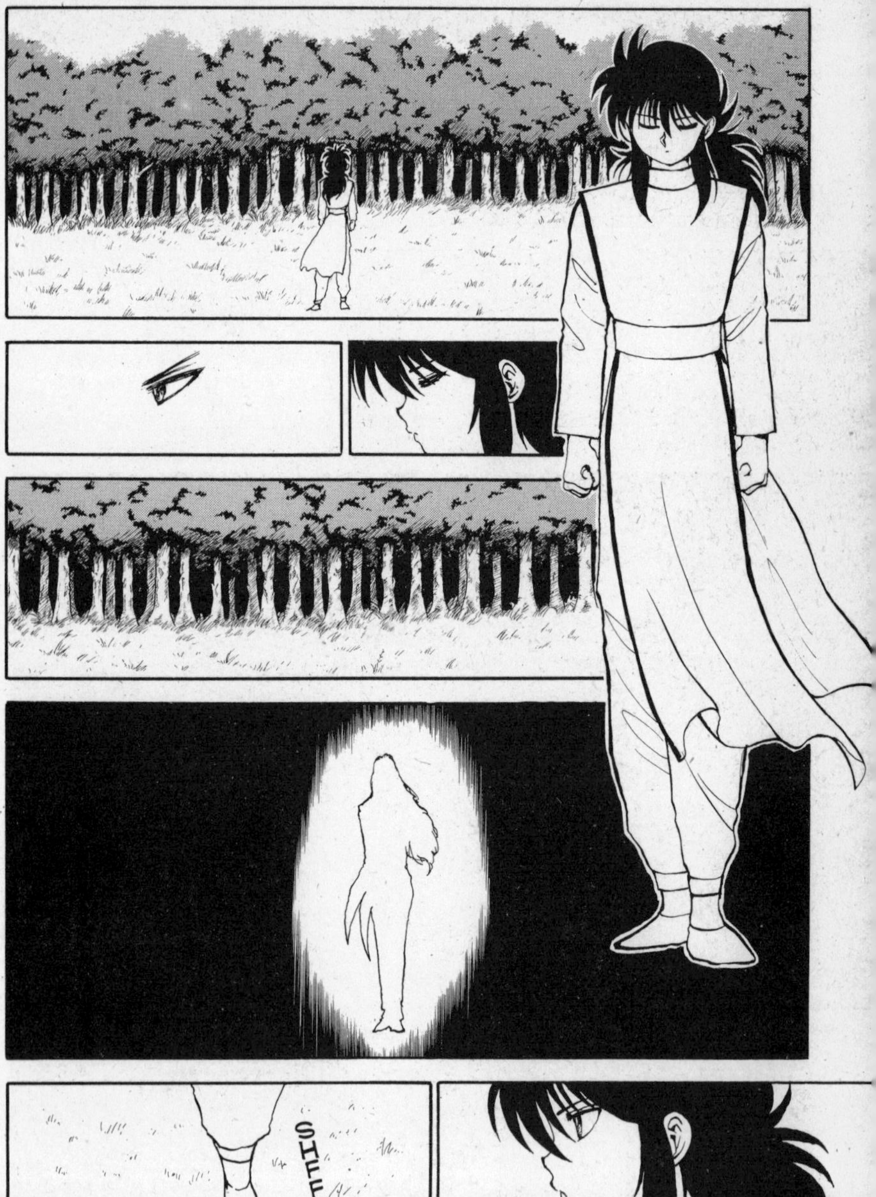
SHFF

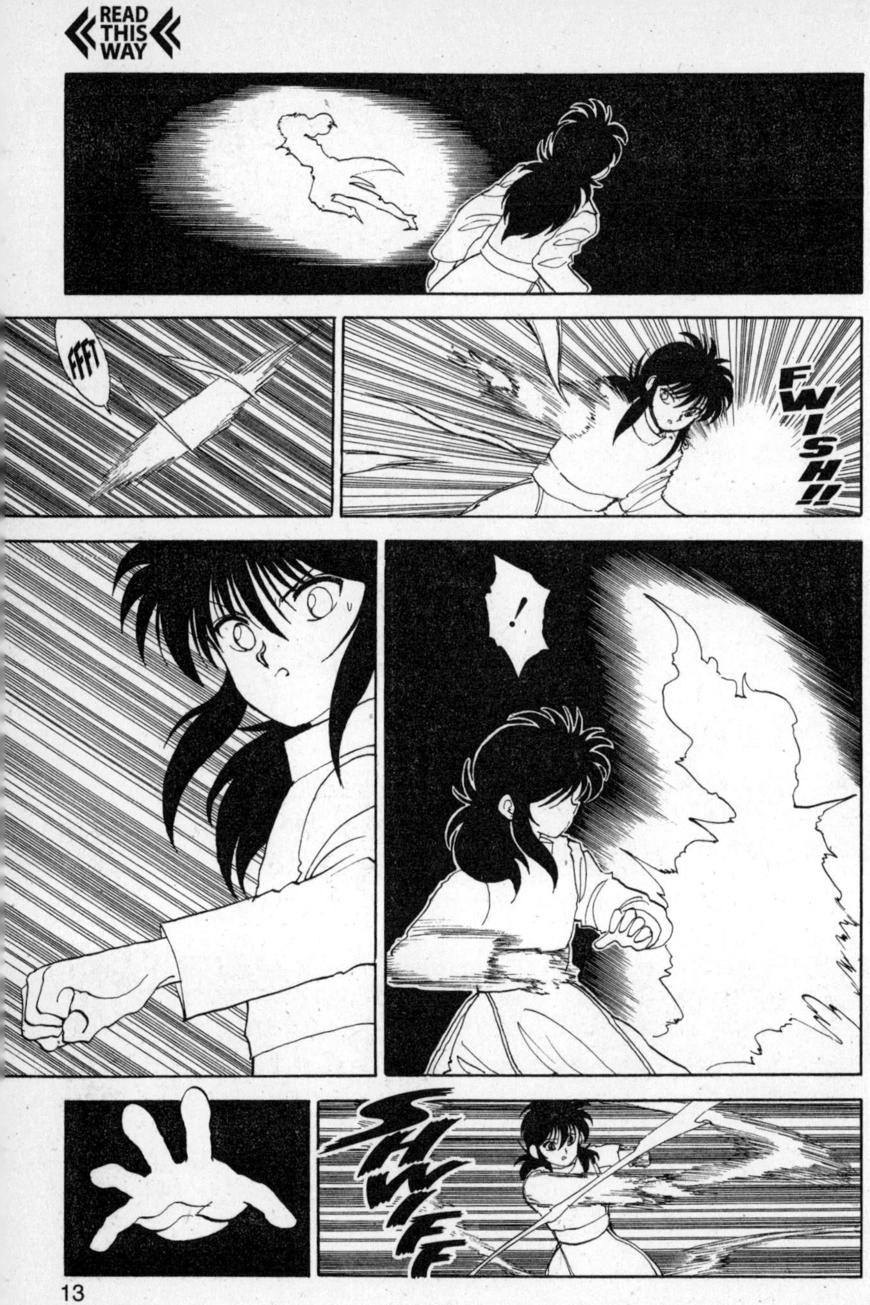
READ THIS WAY
FWISH!!
FFFT
!
SHWIFF

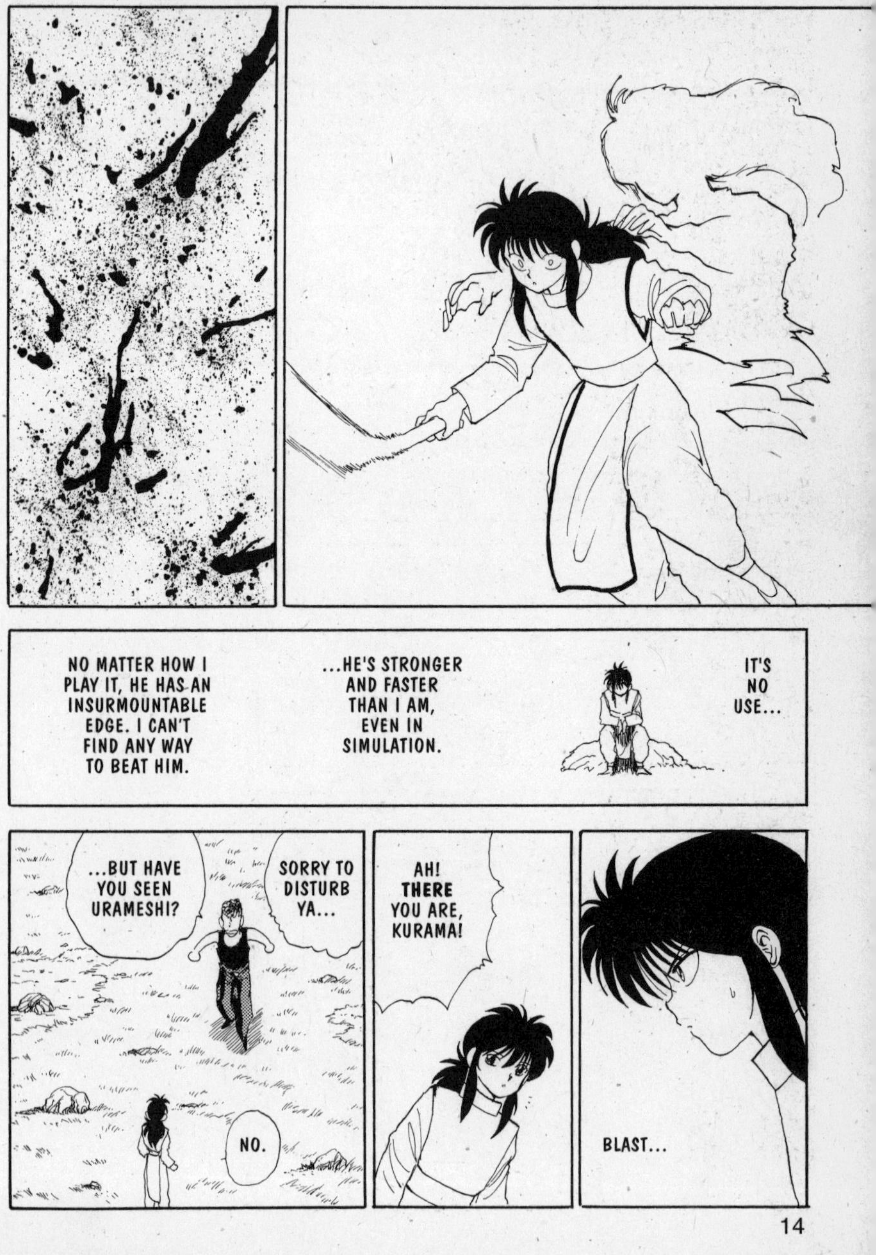

IT'S NO USE...
...HE'S STRONGER AND FASTER THAN I AM, EVEN IN SIMULATION.
NO MATTER HOW I PLAY IT, HE HAS AN INSURMOUNTABLE EDGE. I CAN'T FIND ANY WAY TO BEAT HIM.
BLAST...
AH! **THERE** YOU ARE, KURAMA!
SORRY TO DISTURB YA...
...BUT HAVE YOU SEEN URAMESHI?
NO.

READ THIS WAY

THE MINUTE HE WOKE UP, HE **RACED OFF** LIKE THE DEVIL WAS AFTER HIM. I'VE BEEN LOOKING FOR HIM EVER SINCE!
HUFF
PUFF
OLD GENKAI'S MISSING, TOO. SHE NEVER CAME BACK FROM HER "IMPORTANT BUSINESS."
!
ONE OF YOU WILL DIE TODAY... YOU'LL KNOW WHO...
EH...?
SOMEONE'S **COMING!** IS IT...?
SHUFF
WHO'S THERE?
...
AH...I WAS HOPING I'D FIND YOU TWO ALONE.

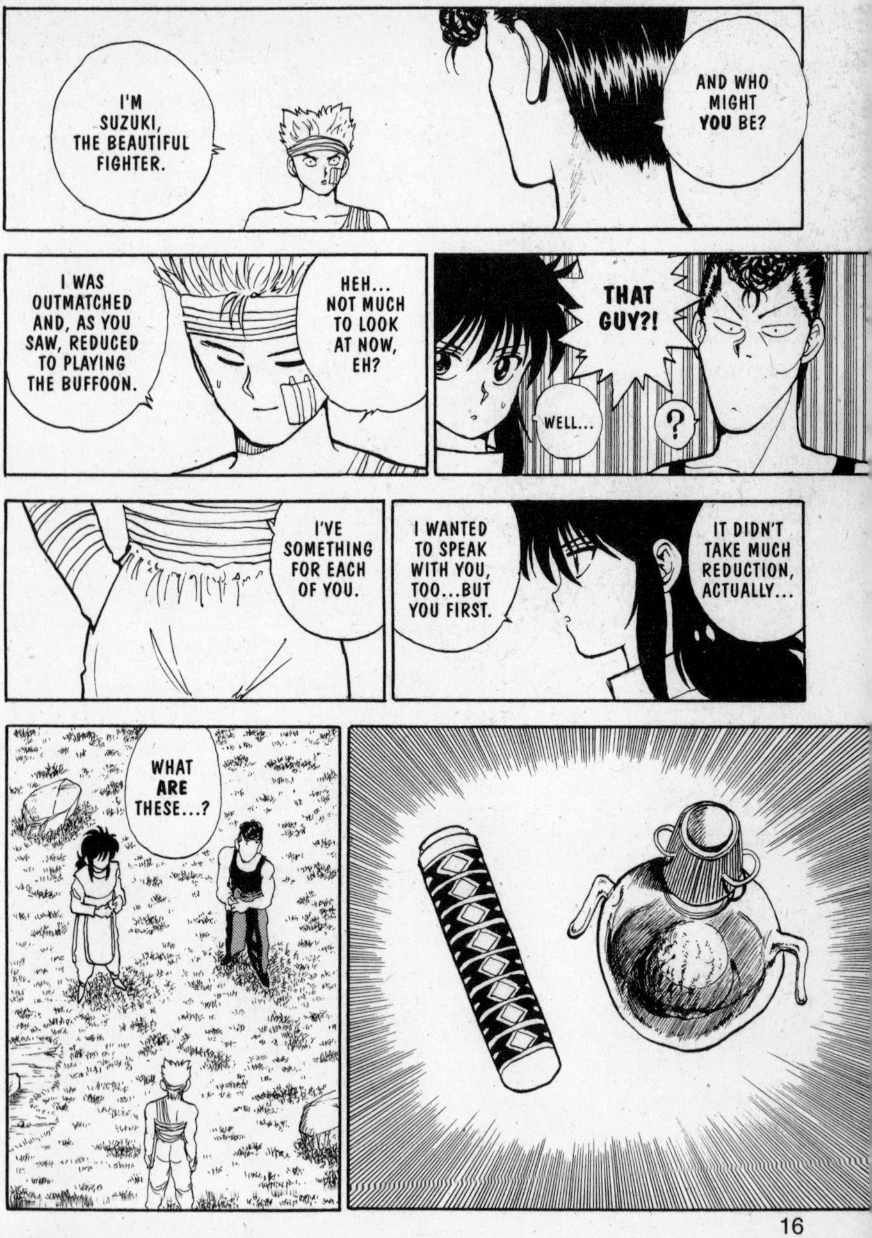
AND WHO MIGHT YOU BE?
I'M SUZUKI, THE BEAUTIFUL FIGHTER.
THAT GUY?!
WELL...
?
HEH... NOT MUCH TO LOOK AT NOW, EH?
I WAS OUTMATCHED AND, AS YOU SAW, REDUCED TO PLAYING THE BUFFOON.
IT DIDN'T TAKE MUCH REDUCTION, ACTUALLY...
I WANTED TO SPEAK WITH YOU, TOO...BUT YOU FIRST.
I'VE SOMETHING FOR EACH OF YOU.
WHAT ARE THESE...?

READ THIS WAY

THE SEED OF DE-INCARNATION AND THE SWORD OF TRIALS.
I'D ORIGINALLY GIVEN THESE TO SHISHIWAKAMARU AND REVERSE URASHIMA.
!!
THE SEED COMES FROM A NEWLY DISCOVERED DEMON PLANE PLANT, THE TIME-EBB FLOWER.
REVERSE URASHIMA USED A VAPOR DERIVATIVE, BUT IF YOU DRINK ITS JUICE IT MIGHT EXTEND YOUR TIME IN DEMON FOX FORM.
THE SWORD OF TRIALS, MADE FROM LEECH CEDAR, IS A VERSATILE WEAPON POWERED BY A PERSON'S CHI. THE BLADE'S APPEARANCE DEPENDS ON THE NATURE OF THE INDIVIDUAL WIELDING IT.
I SHOULD EMPHASIZE THAT BOTH OF THESE ARE UNIQUE DESIGNS, AND HIGHLY EXPERIMENTAL.
I'VE YET TO MAKE A STUDY OF THEIR POTENTIAL SIDE EFFECTS.
USE THEM... OR NOT... AS YOU LIKE.
SEE YA.
WHY GIVE THEM TO US?

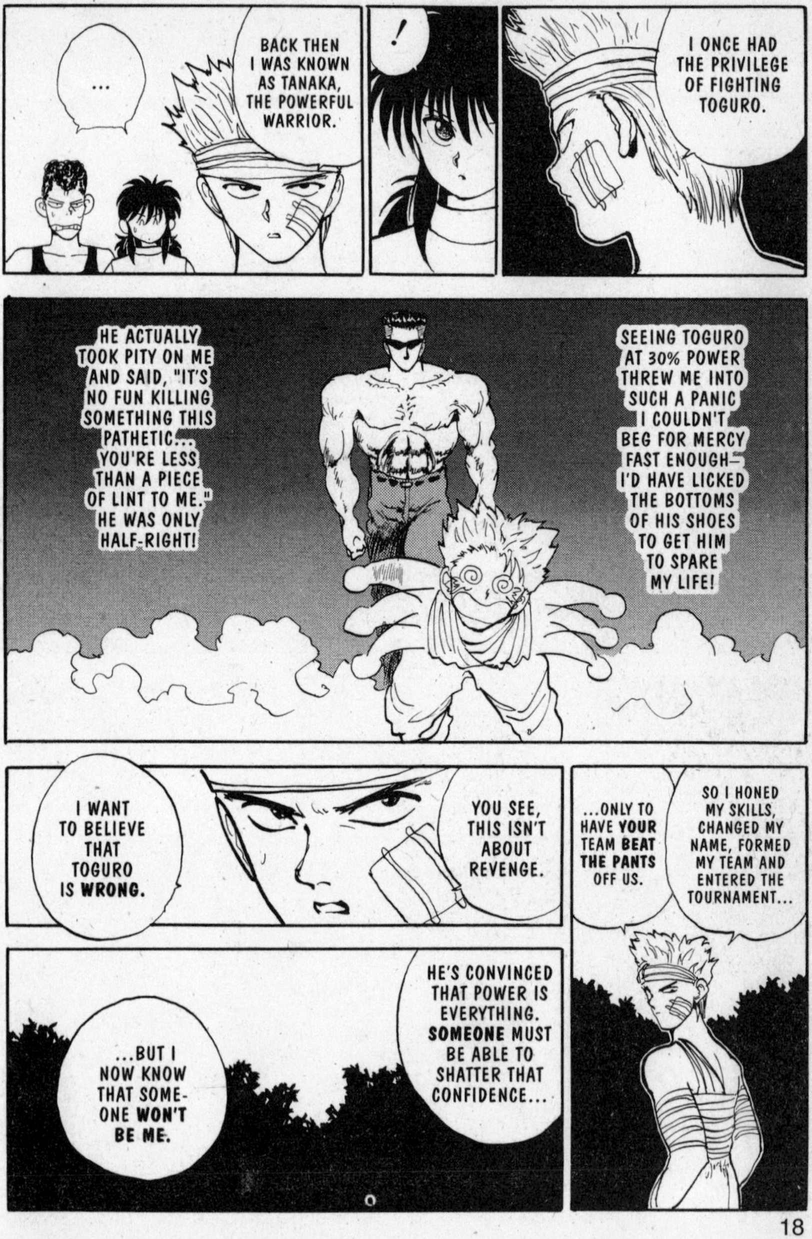
I ONCE HAD THE PRIVILEGE OF FIGHTING TOGURO.
!
BACK THEN I WAS KNOWN AS TANAKA, THE POWERFUL WARRIOR.
...
SEEING TOGURO AT 30% POWER THREW ME INTO SUCH A PANIC I COULDN'T BEG FOR MERCY FAST ENOUGH—I'D HAVE LICKED THE BOTTOMS OF HIS SHOES TO GET HIM TO SPARE MY LIFE!
HE ACTUALLY TOOK PITY ON ME AND SAID, "IT'S NO FUN KILLING SOMETHING THIS PATHETIC... YOU'RE LESS THAN A PIECE OF LINT TO ME." HE WAS ONLY HALF-RIGHT!
SO I HONED MY SKILLS, CHANGED MY NAME, FORMED MY TEAM AND ENTERED THE TOURNAMENT...
...ONLY TO HAVE **YOUR** TEAM **BEAT THE PANTS** OFF US.
YOU SEE, THIS ISN'T ABOUT REVENGE.
I WANT TO BELIEVE THAT TOGURO IS **WRONG.**
HE'S CONVINCED THAT POWER IS EVERYTHING. **SOMEONE** MUST BE ABLE TO SHATTER THAT CONFIDENCE...
...BUT I NOW KNOW THAT SOME-ONE **WON'T BE ME.**

KOENMA...
LOOK, I'M REALLY NOT IN THE MOOD RIGHT NOW...
URK! HOW'D YOU KNOW?
...
EH?
IF I'D BEEN FASTER... GOTTEN THERE SOONER...
BOTAN'S THE SAME WAY. I'D WARNED HER EARLIER THAT GENKAI'S DEATH...
...WAS DRAWING NEAR. HER SENTIMENTAL SIDE OVER-WHELMS HER PROFESSIONALISM SOMETIMES.
I SEE.

YOU? DON'T BE STUPID!!
WHO YOU CALLIN' STUPID?!
WOULD YOU PREFER BONE-HEADED?
EVEN IF YOU HAD BEEN FASTER...
...HOW WOULD YOU HAVE MADE ANY DIFFERENCE?
THEIRS WAS A LIFELONG CLASH OF EGOS...
...AND WHO ARE YOU TO THINK YOU COULD BARGE IN ON THAT?

HM?
WELL?
WANNA LET GO NOW?
...
Jr
OH YEAH... NEARLY FORGOT...
...SHE LEFT ME A MESSAGE FOR YOU.
SHE SAID SHE'S HAD A HECK OF A TIME MAKING ANYTHING OF YOU, AND SHE'S STILL **QUITE DISSATISFIED.**
IN FACT, SHE'S SICK OF YOUR FACE AND WOULD RATHER NOT SEE IT FOR A WHILE.
TWITCH

READ THIS WAY

SO DON'T CROSS OVER, SHE SAID...
...JUST WIN.
.....
FIGURES...
TUMP

YUSUKE?
JUST COMPOSING MY REPLY!
SPECIAL DELIVERY—STRAIGHT TO THE UNDERWORLD!
KIIIIII
YOWZA !!
Jr
BRRRRUMM

TAKE THAT, YA OLD BAT!!
VOOOM

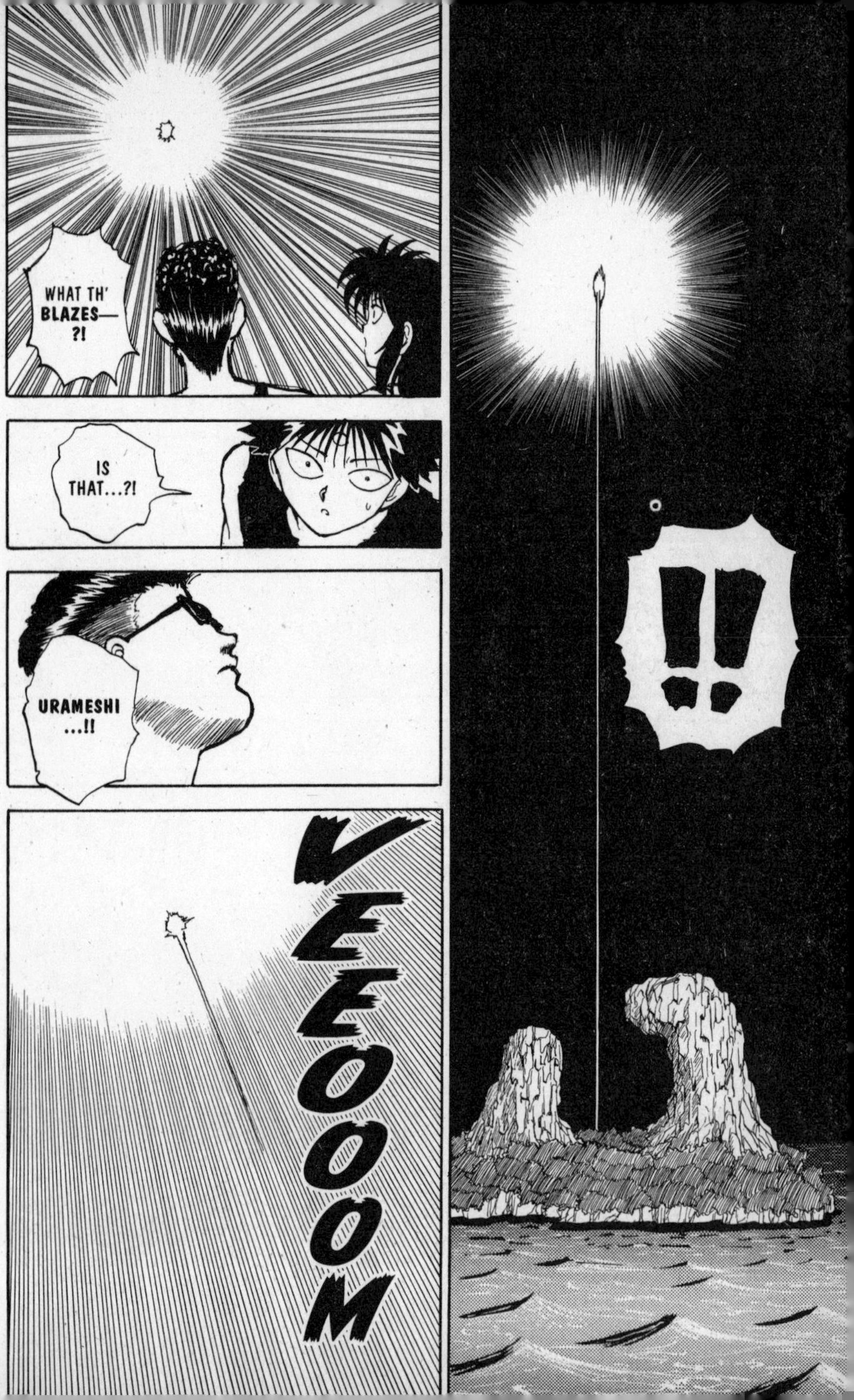
!!
WHAT TH' BLAZES—?!
IS THAT...?!
URAMESHI ...!!
VEEOOOOM

U-UNBELIEV-ABLE!
I'VE NEVER SEEN SUCH POWER!
ANYONE WHO CAN DO THAT... MIGHT JUST BEAT TOGURO!!
THINK IT... REACHED HER?
BROTHER, AND HOW!!
NEXT UP...
THE FINALS!!

HERE'RE THE YUYU HAKUSHO PUZZLES!!
ON WITH YOUR THINKING CAPS!
GET THEM ALL CORRECT AND WIN VALUABLE PRIZES...NOT!!
OH YEAH!
OH YEAH!
HA HA HA HA
IT ALL STARTS ON P.68!!

YOOOOM
ON THIS, THE EVE OF THE TOURNAMENT FINALS...
...WE'RE SEEING A MASSIVE QUEUE FOR GENERAL ADMISSION SEATS.
LET'S CHAT WITH SOME HOPEFUL ATTENDEES!
HI! YOU LOOK COMFY! HOW LONG HAVE YOU BEEN HERE?
TWO WEEKS, MAN.
HAVEN'T YOU BEEN TO THE OTHER MATCHES?!
DO NOT ENTER
SAW 'EM ON TV. IT'S THE FINALS THAT A TRUE FAN'S GOTTA SEE LIVE!
I SNAGGED A NICE MORSEL FROM THE GUEST TOGURO OFFED LAST TIME.
TOMORROW I'LL SECURE THE BEST SEAT SO I CAN MUNCH A CHUNK OF URAMESHI!
YOU WATCHIN' THIS, URAMESHI?! YOU HEARIN' ME?!
YER ON THE MENU TOMORROW, Y'GOT THAT?! TOGURO'LL HAVE YOUR HEAD, AND I'LL RIP THE BRAINS RIGHT FROM YOUR SKULL!!

LEVELING UP!

NAIL URAMESHI, TOGURO!!
KNOCK 'IM OUTTA THE PARK!!
AS YOU CAN SEE, TOGURO'S THE HANDS-DOWN FAVORITE WITH THIS CROWD! AS FOR THOSE OF YOU WATCHING AT HOME...
...YOU CAN CATCH TOMORROW'S FINALS BY TUNING IN...

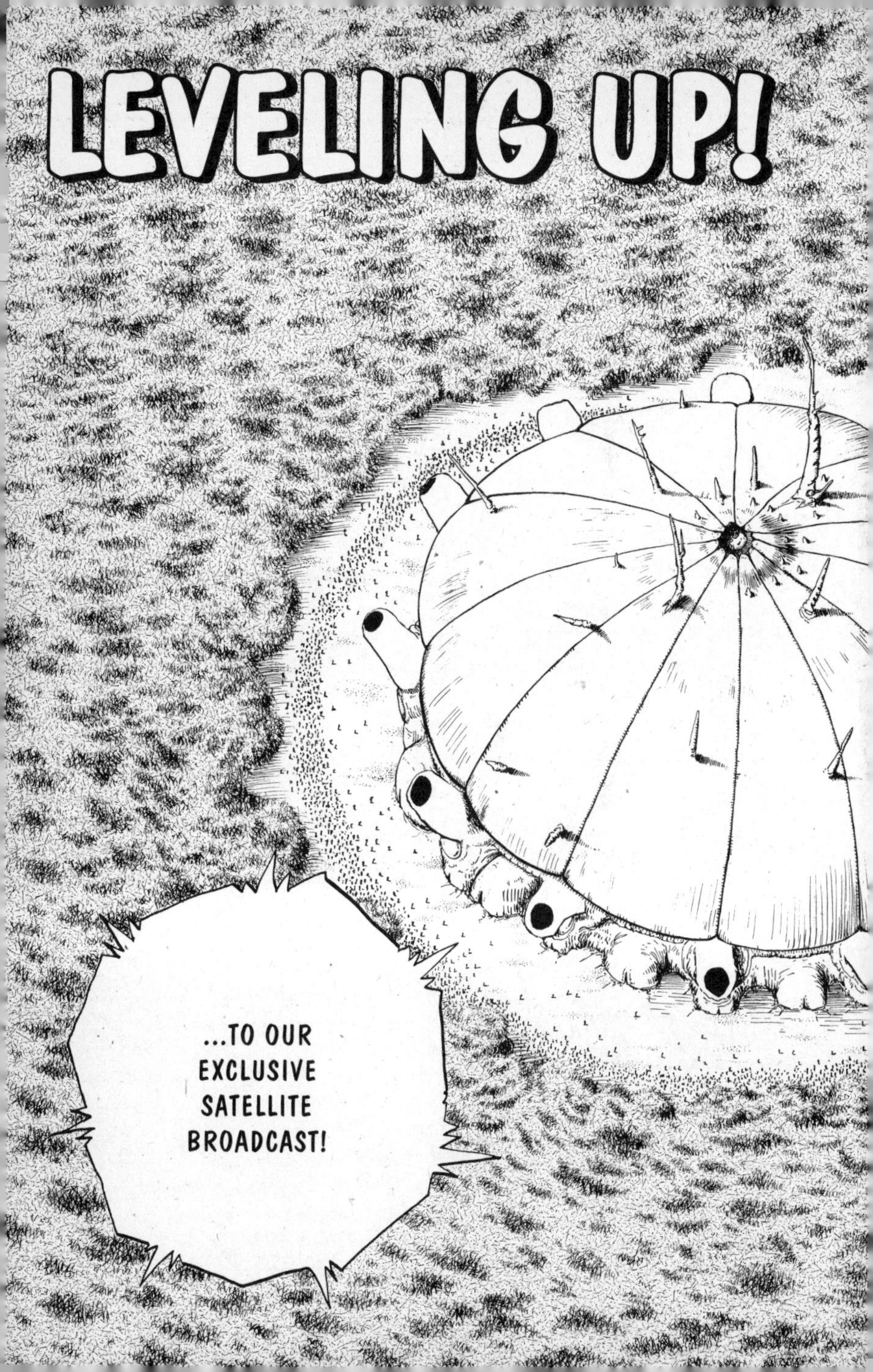
LEVELING UP!
...TO OUR EXCLUSIVE SATELLITE BROADCAST!

I'D SAY IT'S ANOTHER ROUSING SUCCESS, MR. SAKYO.
...!!
...
THAT'S THE PRIVILEGE OF BEING A TEAM OWNER! GUYS LIKE US, WE'LL NEVER SEE A FRACTION OF THAT IN OUR LIFETIMES!
IF IT ALL COMES OUT IN YOUR FAVOR, YOU'LL POCKET 45% OF THE 8 QUADRILLION YEN PROFIT! THAT'S ONE SWEET PAYOFF!
PRIVILEGES: • CHOICE OF THE NEXT SITE • GUEST SELECTION • 45% OF THE PROFITS
I'M THINKING ABOUT IT IN TERMS OF THE HUMAN WORLD.
A PITTANCE LIKE THAT WOULDN'T FINANCE THE CONSTRUCTION OF TOKYO CITY HALL IN THE DEMON PLANE.
WOULD IT HURT TO LET US IN ON THEM?
PREVIOUS OWNERS OF WINNING TEAMS HAVE USED THEIR PRIZE MONEY TO BECOME DICTATORS, OR TO PROBE THE MYSTERIES OF ETERNAL LIFE. YOU, HOWEVER, HAVE KEPT MUM ABOUT YOUR OWN PLANS.

READ THIS WAY

WELL, I WANT TO OPEN A HOLE.
A HOLE...?
WHAT **KIND** OF HOLE?
I'M THINKING A GREAT **BIG** HOLE...
...LIKE A TUNNEL, SET IN PLACE TO LINK THE DEMON PLANE AND THE HUMAN WORLD.
IT'S BEEN SO INCONVENIENT TO RELY ON THE RANDOM AND TRANSITORY DIMENSIONAL DISTORTIONS.
AN ARTIFICIAL ONE COSTS 20 BILLION YEN, AND ONLY GETS YOU A FLEETING, FIST-SIZED APERTURE.
THOSE ARE ONLY GOOD FOR SENDING LESSER DEMONS INTO THE HUMAN WORLD.
IT SCARCELY SEEMS FAIR...
...TO DENY THE BIGGER, STRONGER DEMONS **SIMILAR** ACCESS.

IF REALIZED, THIS TUNNEL, THROUGH WHICH ANY DEMON COULD FREELY PASS...
...WOULD PLUNGE THIS WORLD INTO FAR DEEPER CHAOS.
AN AMUSING PROSPECT, DON'T YOU THINK?
MY COMBINED WINNINGS WOULD PROVIDE SUFFICIENT FUNDING...
...TO FINALLY MAKE THIS DREAM A REALITY.

READ THIS WAY
THE TOURNAMENT IS ONLY POSSIBLE BECAUSE DEMON ACCESS IS LIMITED, AND THEREFORE MANAGEABLE!
IF DEMONS OF ANY TYPE CAN COME THROUGH WHENEVER THEY LIKE, OUR LIVES WON'T BE WORTH SPIT! YOURS EITHER!
THAT'S YOUR PLAN?
YOU CAN'T BE SERIOUS!
BUT YOU SEE, GENTLEMEN...
...THAT'S WHAT MAKES IT INTERESTING.
THAT SETTLES IT! HE'S INSANE!!
WE'VE SUSPECTED IT FOR SOME TIME, FRANKLY!!
SO AS OF THIS MOMENT, WE'RE ASSUMING CONTROL OF THE TOURNAMENT!!
TROMP
TROMP

I THOUGHT THIS MIGHT BE YOUR REACTION.
YOU WERE BETTER OFF NOT KNOWING.
ENOUGH! GET HIM!!

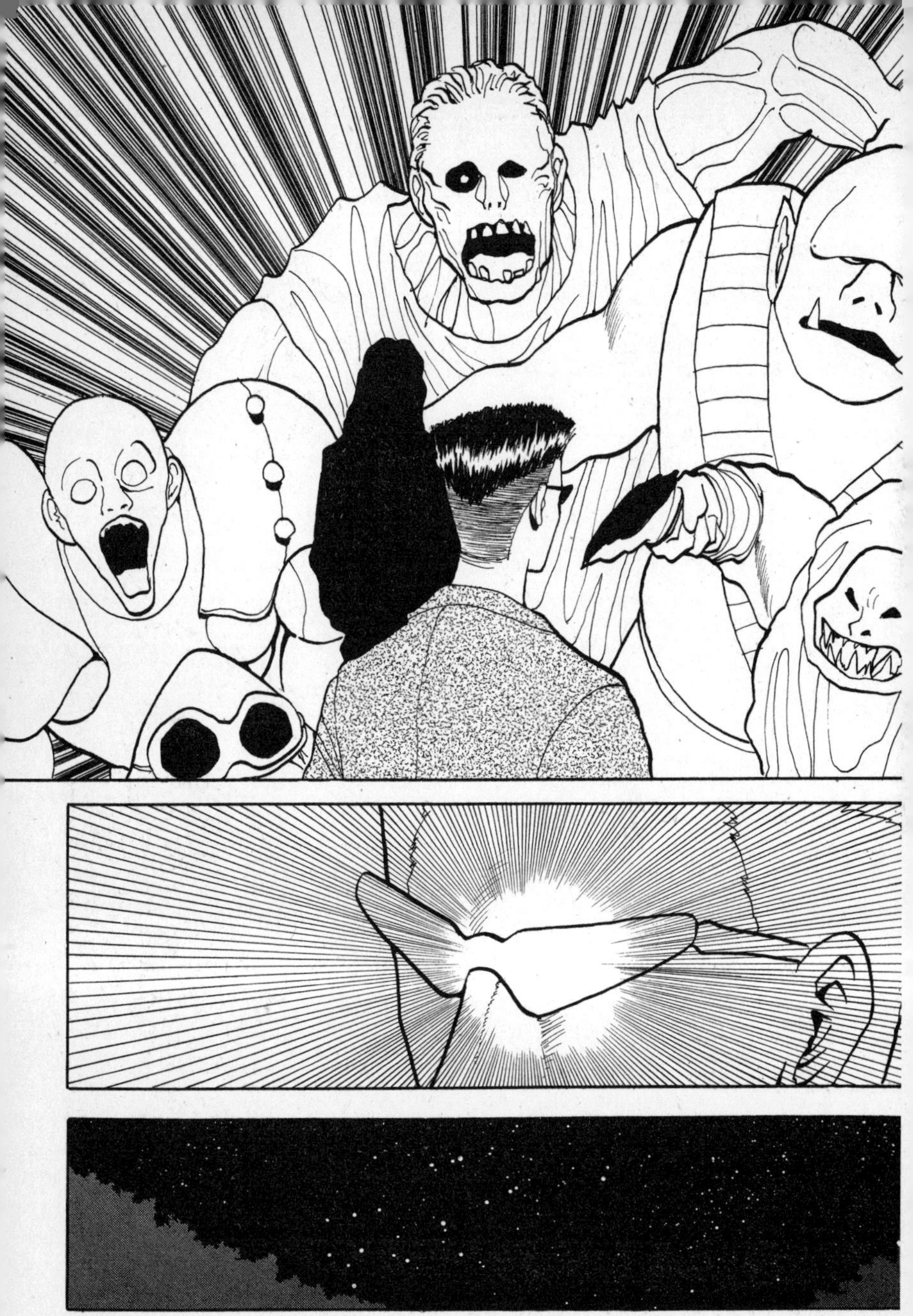

TELL ME, TOGURO... WHAT'S **YOUR** OPINION OF ME?
YOU MAY BE SANE, OR TOTALLY OFF YOUR ROCKER...
...EITHER WAY, I'LL HELP YOU.
YOU SEE, I'VE GOTTEN STRONG... TOO STRONG.
I CAN'T CROSS TO THE DEMON PLANE EVEN THROUGH THE NATURALLY OCCURRING DISTORTIONS.
AND ONCE I DEFEAT URAMESHI...
...THERE WON'T BE ANYONE HERE WORTH FIGHTING. I FIND THAT A VERY DEPRESSING PROSPECT.

READ THIS WAY

AURAS ARE LIKE FINGERPRINTS, UNIQUE TO EACH INDIVIDUAL.
THE BLADE OF THE SWORD OF TRIALS IS FORMED FROM YOUR CHI. IT'LL BE ONE OF A KIND.
AS FOR SIDE EFFECTS... YOUR GUESS IS AS GOOD AS MINE.
...
ONLY ONE THING TO DO... TRY IT!

READ THIS WAY
OKAY, THE HILT'S AN EXTENSION OF MY BODY... FOCUS MY CHI THERE...
SHIFF
FLASH
UNH!!
?!
UNH...
WHOA...
...THAT'S... MY BLADE?!
FEELS LIKE... IT'S SUCKING UP ALL MY ENERGY!!
URGH ...
THLUMP

URAMESHI!!
Y'GOTTA SEE THIS!!
IT'S AWESOME!! SUPER AWESOME!! THE ULTIMATE WEAPON!!
TRUP TRUP TRUP
HOPE YOU'RE PREPARED TO—
CHNK
ULP!
RRRRUMM

PHEW...

THAT AURA FIELD WAS INTENSE!
BET HIS REIGUN'S NOW THE MOST POTENT WEAPON ON EARTH!
OH... HI.
HI YERSELF!
?
DOESN'T MATTER! WE EACH HAVE DIFFERENT CHI!
MINE POWERS A ONE-OF-A-KIND AURA SWORD, Y'KNOW!!
THAT ANY REASON TO BRAY LIKE A WITLESS DONKEY?
HUH?!

READ THIS WAY

HIEI...
MAN, YOUR ARM! IT LOOKS... CRISPED!
THE DRAGON PROVED STUBBORN, SO I HAD TO GET TOUGH.
HA HA... HE'S NUTS, PLAIN NUTS!
SO WHERE'S KURAMA? ANYBODY KNOW?
ACTUALLY, I'VE...
...BEEN HERE A WHILE.
JEEPS! I DIDN'T FEEL HIM, NOT THE TINIEST BIT!
OKAY, THE GANG'S ALL HERE! TO BUSINESS!

YUSUKE TOLD HIS TEAMMATES THAT GENKAI WOULDN'T BE COMING BACK THAT DAY...BUT THAT'S ALL HE WOULD SAY ABOUT IT. NO ONE PRESSED HIM FOR DETAILS, FOR WHICH HE WAS GRATEFUL.
THERE WAS, PERHAPS, SOMETHING IN HIM THAT REFUSED TO CONCEDE TO ANYTHING. PERSONAL EXPERIENCE HAD CERTAINLY CAST DOUBT EVEN ON THE FINALITY OF DEATH. HE WANTED TO BELIEVE THAT GENKAI WOULD BE THERE THE NEXT MORNING, READY AS EVER TO BUST HIS CHOPS OVER SOMETHING!
ONE COULD SENSE THE TRUTH.
ONE STAYED INSIDE HIMSELF.
ONE REMAINED CLUELESS.
EACH, IN HIS WAY, PREPARED HIMSELF FOR WHAT WAS COMING...

AWRIGHT, LET'S GO!!
...THE DAY OF THE FINALS!!
YEAH!

THE RULES RULE!!

TEAM URAMESHI

KURAMA
KAZUMA KUWABARA
HIEI
YUSUKE URAMESHI

DEEP RED RUNS THEIR BLOOD, FAR DEEPER RUNS THEIR BOND!
THEY BATTLE THEIR ENEMIES WITH FIERY GRIT!!

TEAM TOGURO

FROM THE BLACKEST SHADOWS THEY COME, BRINGING THE SCENT OF IMPENDING DOOM! THEIR MENACE IS UNEQUALLED!!

THE RULES RULE!!

WHOOO O

READ THIS WAY

DEATH TO ALL HUMANS!
SNUFF 'EM!
TOGASHI! PAY ME BACK!!
GO FOR 2!

YUSUKE...
...WITH GENKAI GONE...
...WHO'S GOING TO BE OUR FIFTH?
OH, I FOUND SOMEONE.
SO GENKAI'S REALLY OUT OF IT?
I HEARD SOMETHING ABOUT HER GIVING HER POWERS TO YUSUKE. GUESS SHE USED HERSELF UP IN THE SEMIFINALS, EH?
SHEESH...
...YOU REALLY ARE CLUELESS.
WHY YOU LITTLE—
HELLO, EVERYONE, AND THANK YOU FOR YOUR PATIENCE! SORRY FOR THE DELAY, BUT NOW...
EEP!

READ THIS WAY

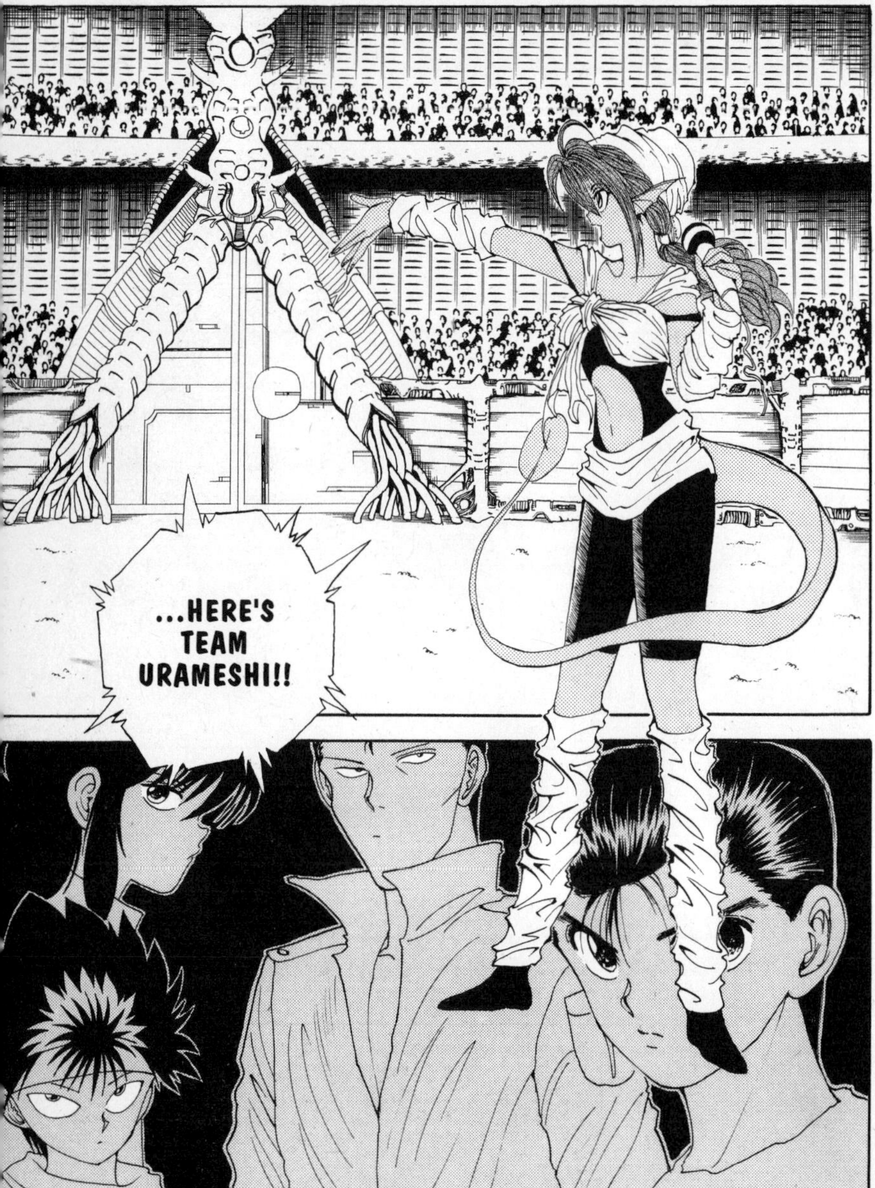
...HERE'S TEAM URAMESHI!!

THE NERVE OF 'EM EVEN SHOWING UP!
DIE, YOU BUGS! DIE!!
FILTHY HUMANS!!
MY MONEY'S ON YOU ALL BUYING IT, SO YOU'D BETTER!!
IF YOU KNOW WHAT'S GOOD FOR YOU!!

READ THIS WAY
AND PRESENTING... TEAM TOGURO!
DOOOM!
YOU GO, TOGURO! MASSACRE 'EM!!
GIVE 'EM SUCH A THUMPING !!
OOOO

RAAH
RAAH
RAAH
RAAH
MURMUR
MURMUR
RAAH
RAAH
BZZZ

READ THIS WAY
BZZZ
YAMMER
YAMMER
HUH? ONLY FOUR ON EACH TEAM?!
WHAT'S THE DEAL HERE?!
QUIET PLEASE!
ACCORDING TO TOURNAMENT RULES...
RULES
...THE FINALS ARE STRICTLY ONE-ON-ONE! WHICHEVER TEAM...
...TAKES THREE OUT OF FIVE MATCHES WILL BE DECLARED THE WINNER!!
NATTER
MUTTER
MURMUR

IF A TEAM SUFFERS NO FATALITIES, THEN...
...A FIFTH MEMBER MUST BE CALLED IN!
SO WHO'S OUR FIFTH, HUH?! JIN? CHU?
HOPE HE DIDN'T CHICKEN OUT...
WE'VE ALREADY HIT A SNAG, FOLKS!
NO WAY TO SAY JUST HOW THINGS WILL GO TODAY!
C'MON, BRING OUT YOUR FIFTHS! NOW!
RAAH
RAAH
WE'RE SICK OF WAITING!!

READ THIS WAY
ALL RIGHT, WE'LL BRING HIM OUT.
RRRRRUM
RR
OOOOH
HEY! ISN'T THAT THE TEAM OWNER?
NITTER NATTER
THINK SO... BUT CAN HE FIGHT?

FIGHTING'S NOT MY THING, ACTUALLY.
BUT I'LL ENJOY A CLOSE-UP VIEW OF TEAM URAMESHI'S DEMISE.
BELIEVE ME, THERE'S NO CHANCE I'LL...
...BE NEEDED.
SAKYO'S DECLARING VICTORY ALREADY!!
HE'S CONFIDENT. THAT'S NICE.
LOOM!!

READ THIS WAY

KOENMA ?!
HAD TO SHOW OFF, HUH?
THOSE WHO GOVERN THE UNDERWORLD SHOULD AVOID GETTING INVOLVED IN AFFAIRS LIKE THIS...
...BUT CURRENT CIRCUMSTANCES FORCE ME TO STEP **OUTSIDE** THOSE BOUNDS, AND INTO THIS ARENA.
IN THE UNLIKELY EVENT...
...IT COMES DOWN TO ME AND WHOEVER...
FWAP
...I'VE GOT AN **ESCAPE PLAN** ALL FIGURED OUT!
BOOSTER ROCKETS!!
HE **SERIOUS?**
NEVER NEEDED HIM...

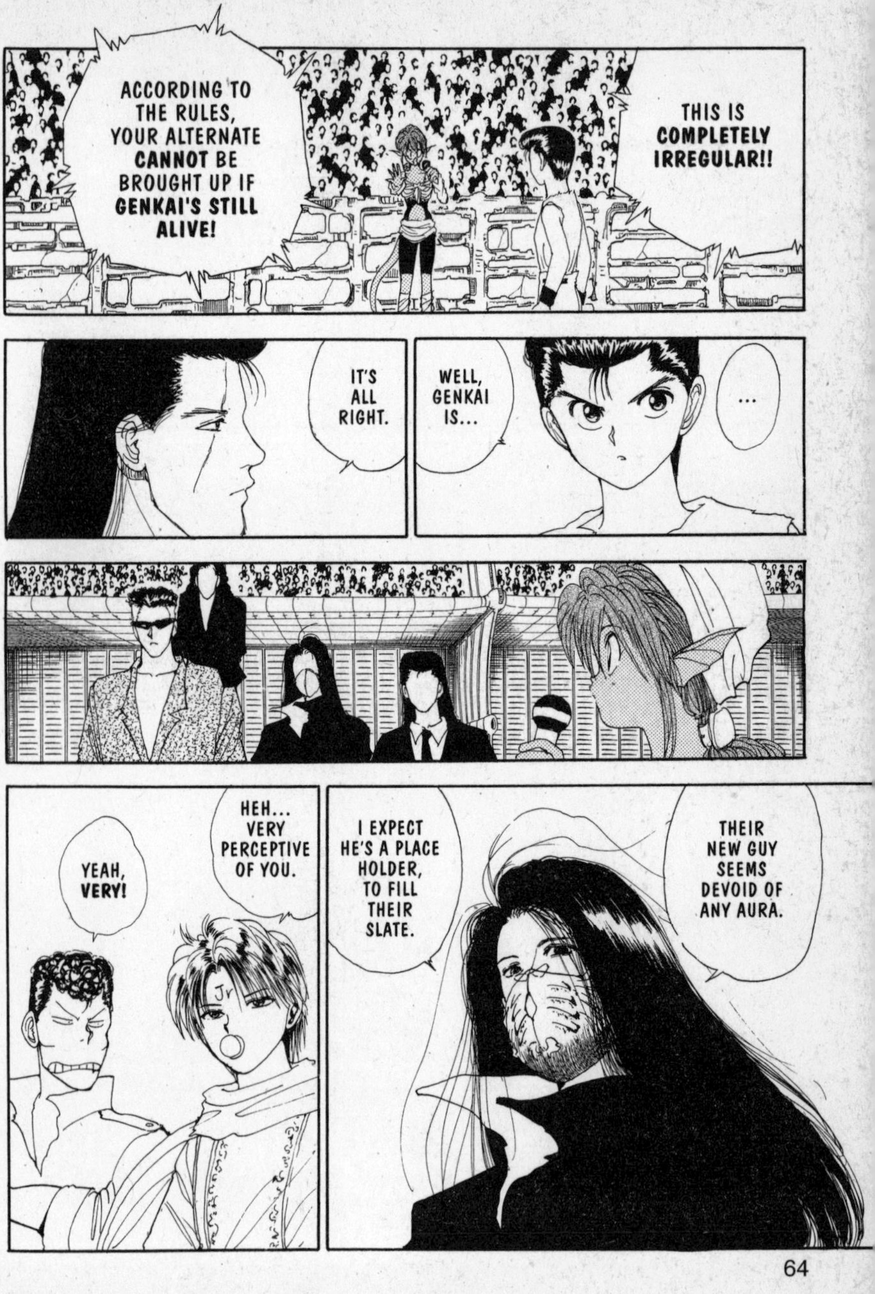
THIS IS **COMPLETELY IRREGULAR!!**
ACCORDING TO THE RULES, YOUR ALTERNATE **CANNOT BE** BROUGHT UP IF **GENKAI'S STILL ALIVE!**
...
WELL, GENKAI IS...
IT'S ALL RIGHT.
THEIR NEW GUY SEEMS DEVOID OF ANY AURA.
I EXPECT HE'S A PLACE HOLDER, TO FILL THEIR SLATE.
HEH... VERY PERCEPTIVE OF YOU.
YEAH, **VERY!**

Jr
HERE ARE OUR TEN FINALISTS!!

IT'S STARTING AT LAST!
YEAH
RAAH
RAAH
RAAH
I'LL TAKE HIM.
BANG!

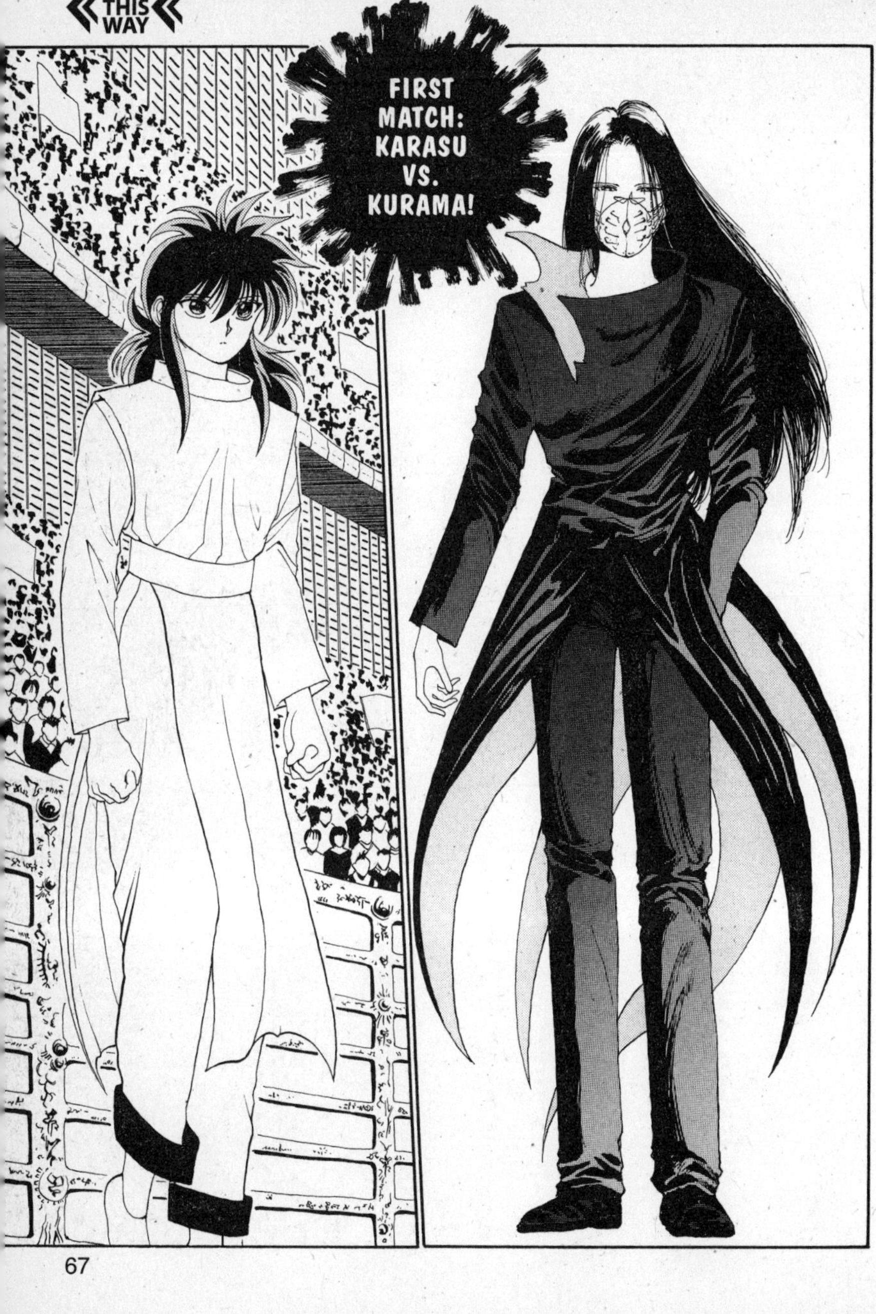
FIRST MATCH: KARASU VS. KURAMA!

YUYU HAKUSHO PUZZLES: ①

ELIMINATE THE LETTERS IN THE BUBBLES BELOW IN THE ORDER THEY APPEAR IN THE ANIME OPENING LYRICS. WHICH OF THE FIVE CHARACTERS HAS THE LAST LETTER REMAINING?

-IGNORE LETTERS WITH SONANT MARKS, LIKE "GA" AND "ZA."
-SPELL KANJI OUT INTO HIRAGANA.
-BEGIN WITH THE TITLE.
("HOHOEMI NO BAKUDAN" <-CROSS OFF E, NO, AND KU
["A SMILE THAT'S A BOMB" <- CROSS OFF A, M, I, ETC.])

THE INVISIBLE FEAT!!

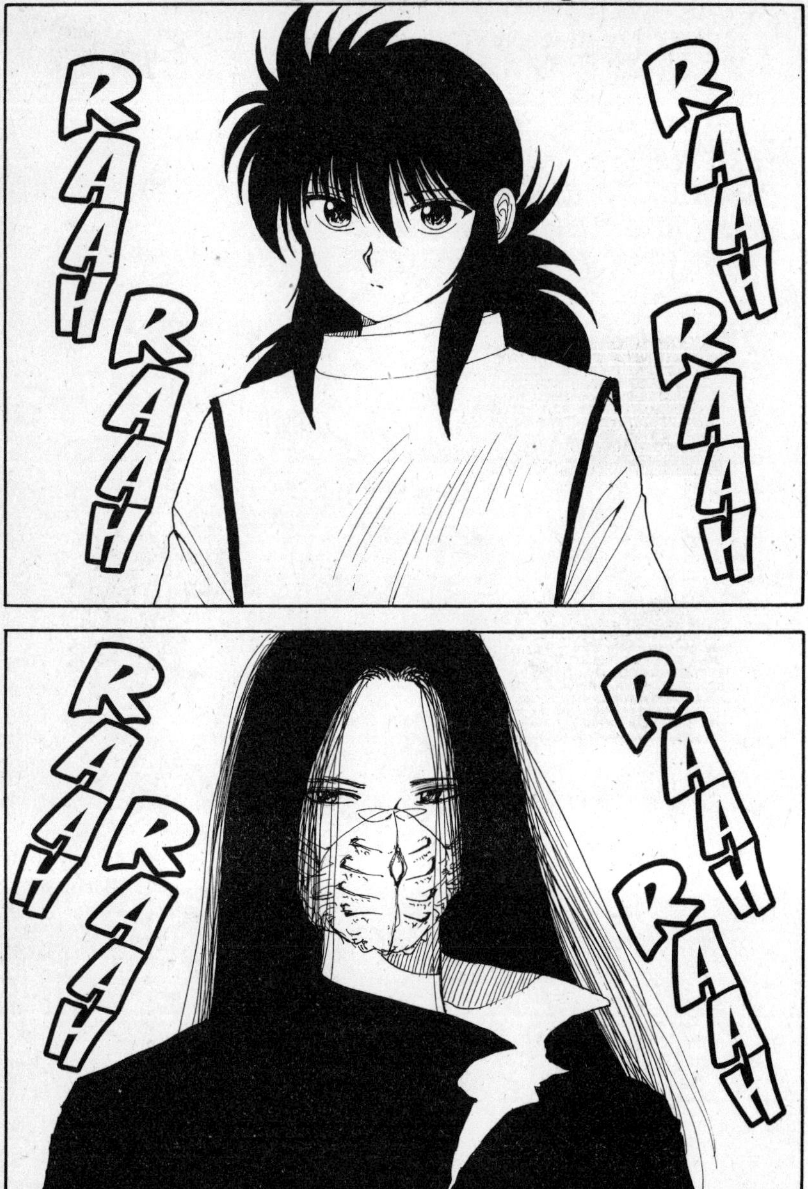

THE INVISIBLE FEAT!!

READ THIS WAY

HEY, KURAMA, YOU GONNA...
...USE THAT... UH, FRUIT JUICE...
... SUZUKI GAVE YOU?
YES.
I HAD SOME TWO MINUTES AGO.
WHAT?
I TRIED IT A FEW TIMES...
...AND FOUND THE LIQUID FORM TAKES A LITTLE WHILE TO WORK.
Y'MEAN YOU'VE **TRIED** IT... MORE'N **ONCE?**
OF COURSE. PRACTICE MAKES PERFECT, Y'KNOW.
AND SUZUKI WAS RIGHT...
...ONE SIP, AND I CAN HOLD MY OLD FORM FOR 15 MINUTES.
THAT **SHOULD** BE ENOUGH TIME.

FORWARD!!
RAAH
RAAH
KARASU!!
RAAH
BUTCHER 'IM!!
RAAH
RAAH
THE OPENING MATCH IS ABOUT TO START!
THE STADIUM'S ERUPTING WITH WILD CHEERING FOR TEAM TOGURO'S KARASU!!
HEY! THERE'S TEAM URAMESHI ROOTERS HERE, TOO!
NAIL 'IM, KURAMA!

READ THIS WAY

SHOULD WE EVEN BE HERE? I HEAR IT CAN GET REALLY ROUGH DURING THE FINALS.
TUT TUT... THE GUYS NEED OUR SUPPORT. WE CAN HANDLE THIS CROWD.
HOW'D WE GET SUCH GOOD SEATS?
LET'S JUST SAY WE RAN INTO A GENEROUS SCALPER.
SEE YUYU HAKUSHO VOL. 6, P.172-3.
GENKAI... WHERE'S GENKAI?
I DON'T SEE HER! WHY ISN'T SHE IN THE RING?
DID SHE WEAR HER-SELF OUT IN THE SEMI-FINALS?
WHADDAYA THINK, BOTAN?
HUH? ME? I, UH...
...HEARD HER SAY YOU CAN'T FIGHT OLD AGE.
SO WHERE YOU GOIN'? IT'S ABOUT TO START.
GOTTA... PICK FLOWERS... OR SOME-THING...
?
SHE'S SURE BEEN ACTING ODD.
...

PAT
CHEER UP, BOTAN.
SHIZURU?
HOW'LL SHE EVER REST IN PEACE...
...IF YOU, THE GUIDE, GET ALL MOPEY?
Y'MEAN... YOU KNOW?
I'VE KNOWN HER FOR SOME TIME, AND...
...YESTER-DAY, HER SPIRIT...
...DROPPED BY TO SAY GOODBYE.
SHE DIDN'T SAY ANYTHING ABOUT... THE END, BUT SHE SEEMED CONTENT.
DEATH'S NO BIG DEAL FOR HER, I THINK.
...
YEAH...

READ THIS WAY
...BUT...
...BUT IT'S A BIG DEAL TO ME!!
TELL YA WHAT, LET'S LEAVE IT TO THE GUYS...
...AND IF THEY GET TROUNCED, I'LL PUT TEAM TOGURO DOWN MYSELF!
DON'T SAY THAT... Y'MIGHT JINX 'EM!
RAAH
SNIFF
RAAH RAAH
RAAH RAAH
RAAH
OOOOH
BEGIN!!

IS THAT HOW YOU WANT TO FACE ME?
YOU'RE NOT HERE TO JUST THROW YOUR LIFE AWAY, I HOPE.
IT'S NONE OF YOUR BUSINESS...
...HOW I CHOOSE TO FACE YOU...

...AND DEFEAT YOU.
SHEER BLUFF, BUT I NEED TO BUY SOME TIME.
WHATEVER HAPPENS, I CAN'T LET HIM TOUCH ME.

FLICK!
FLICK!
FLOOOSH
KURAMA SEEMS TO HAVE RAISED A SHIELD OF... FLOWER PETALS?
FWIISH
KARASU'S STROLLING RIGHT INTO THE THICK OF IT!!

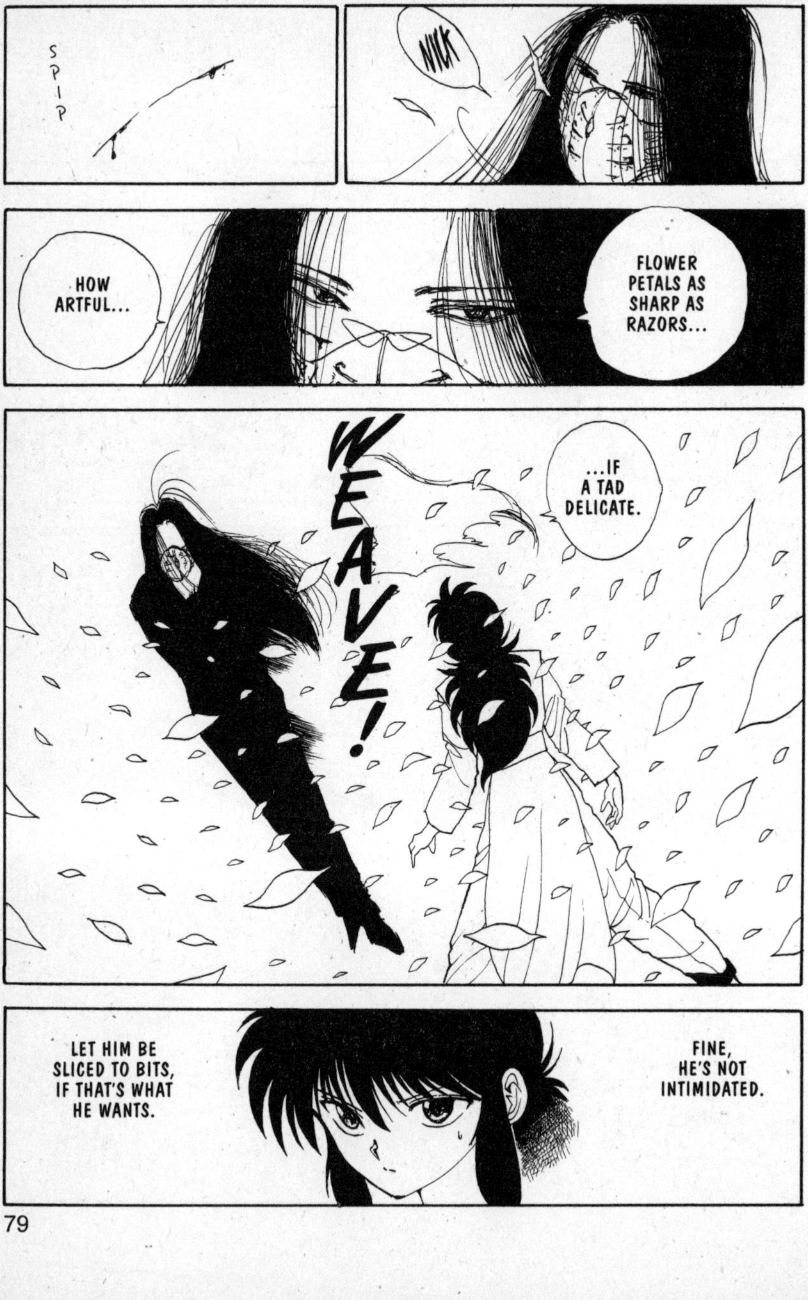
NICK
SPIP
FLOWER PETALS AS SHARP AS RAZORS...
HOW ARTFUL...
...IF A TAD DELICATE.
WEAVE!
FINE, HE'S NOT INTIMIDATED.
LET HIM BE SLICED TO BITS, IF THAT'S WHAT HE WANTS.

WOOOSH
BWOOM
BWOOM
HUH?!

READ THIS WAY

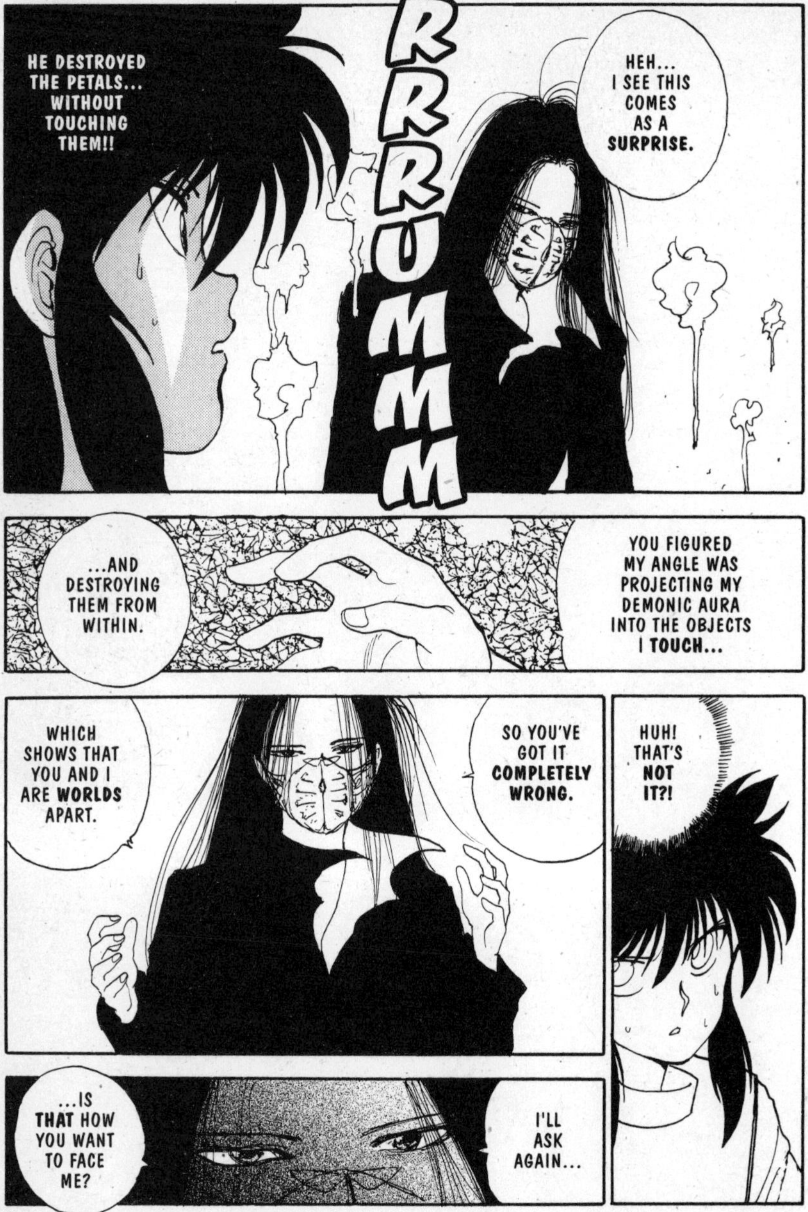
HEH... I SEE THIS COMES AS A SURPRISE.
RRRUMMM
HE DESTROYED THE PETALS... WITHOUT TOUCHING THEM!!
YOU FIGURED MY ANGLE WAS PROJECTING MY DEMONIC AURA INTO THE OBJECTS I TOUCH...
...AND DESTROYING THEM FROM WITHIN.
SO YOU'VE GOT IT COMPLETELY WRONG.
HUH! THAT'S NOT IT?!
WHICH SHOWS THAT YOU AND I ARE WORLDS APART.
I'LL ASK AGAIN...
...IS THAT HOW YOU WANT TO FACE ME?

!!
SKSSH
UNH!
BWAM!
AAH!
GUUH...!!
SLUMP

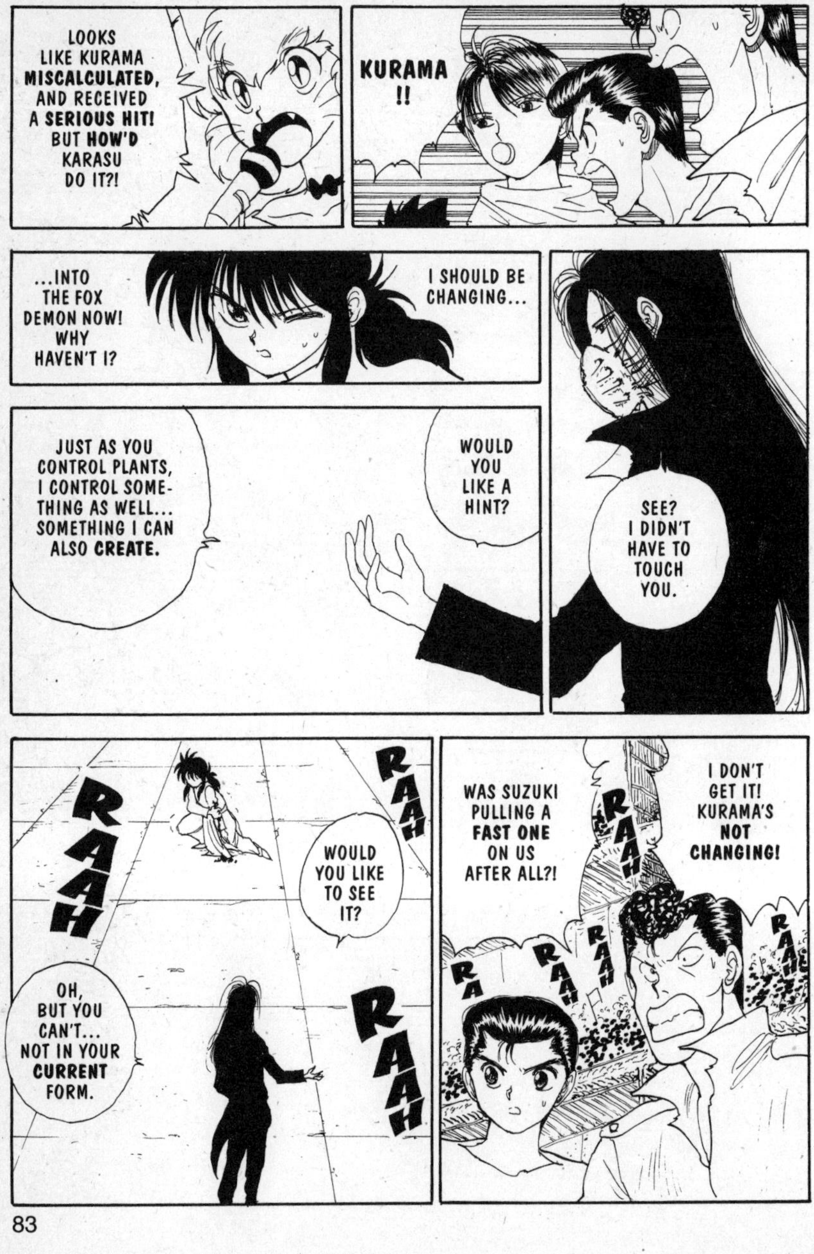
KURAMA !!
LOOKS LIKE KURAMA MISCALCULATED, AND RECEIVED A SERIOUS HIT! BUT HOW'D KARASU DO IT?!
SEE? I DIDN'T HAVE TO TOUCH YOU.
I SHOULD BE CHANGING...
...INTO THE FOX DEMON NOW! WHY HAVEN'T I?
WOULD YOU LIKE A HINT?
JUST AS YOU CONTROL PLANTS, I CONTROL SOME-THING AS WELL... SOMETHING I CAN ALSO CREATE.
I DON'T GET IT! KURAMA'S NOT CHANGING!
WAS SUZUKI PULLING A FAST ONE ON US AFTER ALL?!
RAAH
RAAH
RAAH
RAAH
RA
RAAH
WOULD YOU LIKE TO SEE IT?
RAAH
RAAAH
OH, BUT YOU CAN'T... NOT IN YOUR CURRENT FORM.

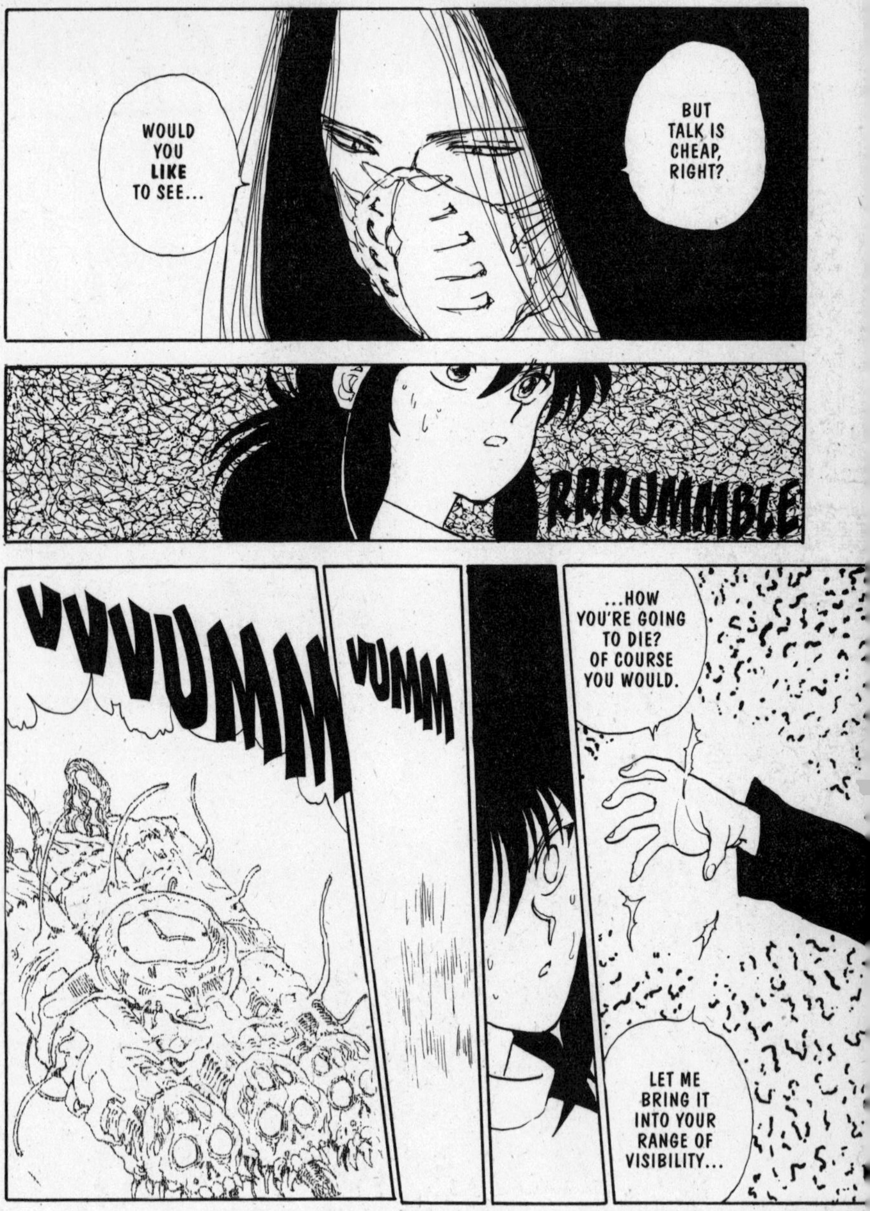
BUT TALK IS CHEAP, RIGHT?
WOULD YOU LIKE TO SEE...
RRRUMMBLE
...HOW YOU'RE GOING TO DIE? OF COURSE YOU WOULD.
LET ME BRING IT INTO YOUR RANGE OF VISIBILITY...
VUMM
VVVUMM

FAH
FOOM
WHAT THE...?
THAT'S RIGHT... A BOMB!!
KA-BOOM

KURAMA!!
OW!
PLIP
LAST ACT OF DEFIANCE ...
NEARLY THE LAST.
SHUICHI MINAMINO WOULD'VE BEEN VAPORIZED ...

READ THIS WAY

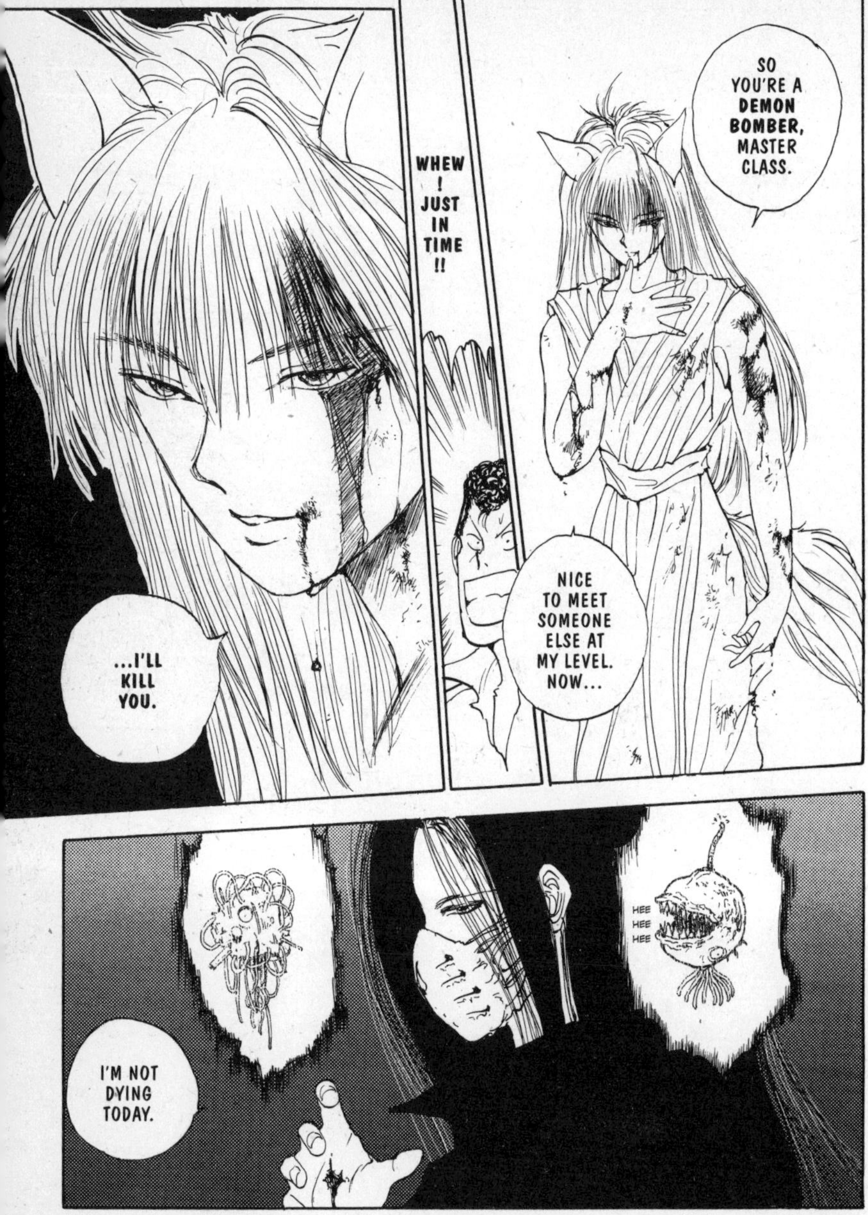

SO YOU'RE A DEMON BOMBER, MASTER CLASS.
NICE TO MEET SOMEONE ELSE AT MY LEVEL. NOW...
WHEW! JUST IN TIME!!
...I'LL KILL YOU.
HEE HEE HEE
I'M NOT DYING TODAY.

YUYU HAKUSHO PUZZLES: ②

THE FOUR GUYS PLAYED MAHJONG.
BASED ON THEIR STATEMENTS,
ANSWER THE TWO QUESTIONS.

- ONLY ONE OF THEM IS LYING.
- THE OTHER THREE ARE TELLING THE TRUTH.

I WAS NOT ABLE TO WIN.
I LOST TO YUSUKE, BUT I BEAT HIEI.
I DIDN'T FINISH LAST, BY THE WAY.
ONLY HIEI AND KUWABARA LOST TO ME.

① WHICH ONE OF THEM IS LYING?

② IN WHAT ORDER DID THEY PLACE?

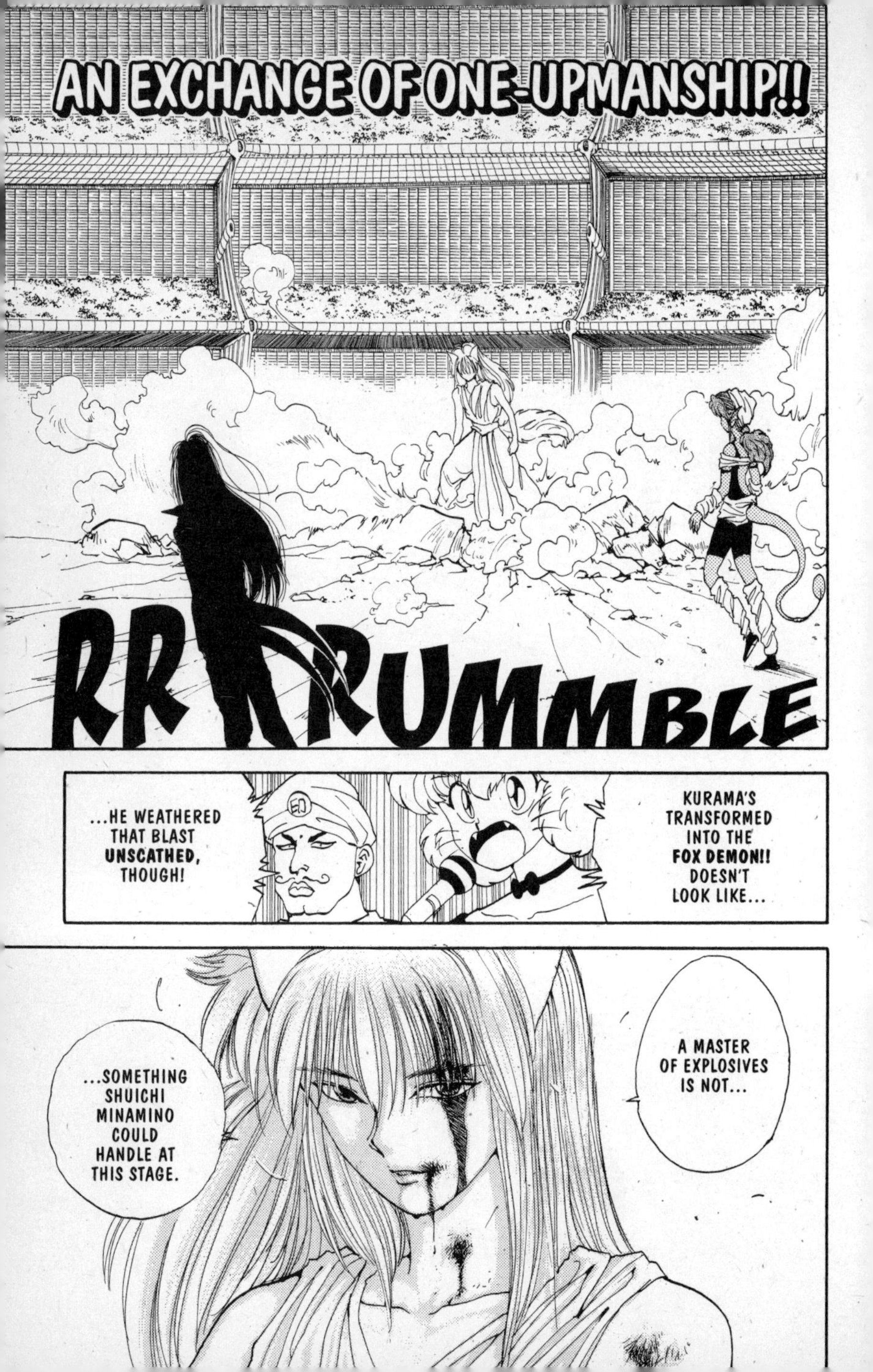
AN EXCHANGE OF ONE-UPMANSHIP!!
RRRRUMMBLE
KURAMA'S TRANSFORMED INTO THE FOX DEMON!! DOESN'T LOOK LIKE...
...HE WEATHERED THAT BLAST UNSCATHED, THOUGH!
A MASTER OF EXPLOSIVES IS NOT...
...SOMETHING SHUICHI MINAMINO COULD HANDLE AT THIS STAGE.

AN EXCHANGE OF ONE-UPMANSHIP!!

RAAH
RAAH
RAAH
HEH HEH... IS THAT HOW YOU'LL EXCUSE LOSING?
BECAUSE YOU'RE GOING TO, EVEN IN THAT FORM!
SHLORP
CRICK
CRACK
CRACKLE
AND HERE'S HOW.
FWISS

SKREEE
TRACER EYES: SUB-ORGANISMS SPAWNED BY MY DEMONIC AURA.
AS YOU KNOW, WHAT A MASTER ENVISIONS, HE CAN CREATE.
BWOOOM
BWOOOM

FWISH
FWISH
EVER HEAR OF THE HUMBLE PLANT, BY CHANCE?
IT'S A SOUTH AMERICAN PERENNIAL THAT CLOSES ITS LEAVES WHEN TOUCHED BY HAND OR FIRE.
HORTI-CULTURE'S NOT MY THING.
NOTE THAT YOU'RE HEMMED IN.
IN FACT, I'D SAY YOU'RE IN A BIT OF A FIX.

PERHAPS. BACK TO THE HUMBLE PLANT...
WHOOSH
WHOA!

KREE
KREE
THE DEMON PLANE VARIETY HAS A VICIOUS TEMPER-AMENT.
IT'LL ATTACK ANYTHING THAT MOVES OR EMITS EXCESSIVE HEAT.
THAT MEANS YOU, WOMAN. IF YOU WISH TO LIVE, STAY STILL!
WELL NOW, I'D SAY IT'S FOUND AN ENEMY.
KREEK
STIFF
YOU BET.
FROZEN

SKREEE!!
THERE'S NO ESCAPE, I'M AFRAID.
UNH!
SMASH!
BASH!

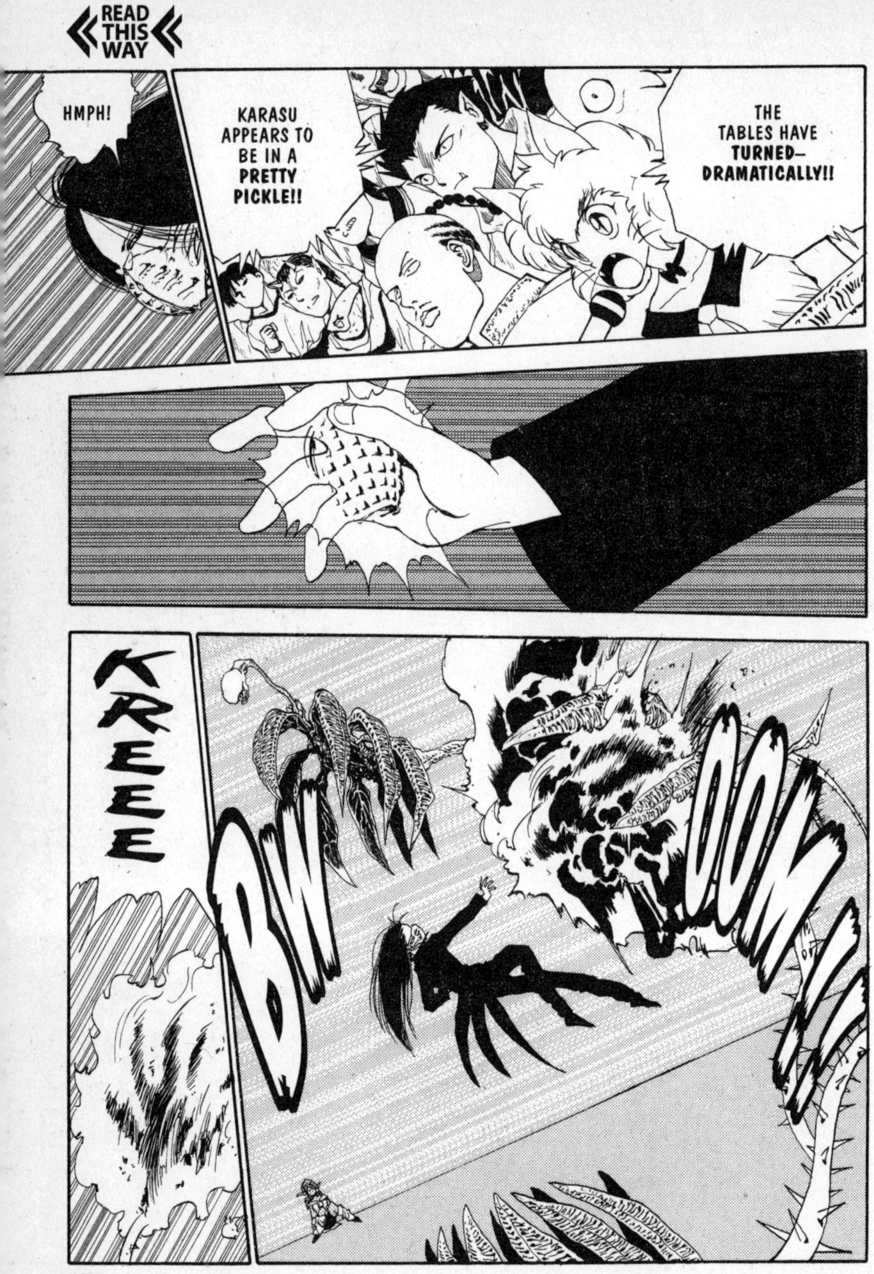

READ THIS WAY
THE TABLES HAVE TURNED— DRAMATICALLY!!
KARASU APPEARS TO BE IN A PRETTY PICKLE!!
HMPH!
BWOOM
KREEE

SKSSSH
PARTIAL ATTACKS WON'T DO MUCH, I'M AFRAID.
BANG

WHO'S OUT OF COM-MISSION?
NO ONE, KARASU! CERTAINLY NOT YOU!
LET THE MATCH RESUME!!
I'VE TAKEN QUITE A LIKING TO YOU, KURAMA.
I'LL SEE YOU DEAD FOR SURE!
HIS MASK CAME OFF.
NOT GOOD.
GET BEHIND ME, MR. SAKYO... QUICKLY.
KAAAH!

...HE'D HAVE MORE FIGHT IN HIM.
AMAZING!! LOOKS LIKE THIS MATCH GOES TO KURAMA!!
AS THE FOX DEMON, HE'S PROVED OVER-WHELMING!!
WAY T'GO, KURAMA!!
THAT DIDN'T EVEN TAKE THE WHOLE 15 MINUTES!!
WITH KARASU OUT OF COMMISSION...
...THE MATCH GOES TO—

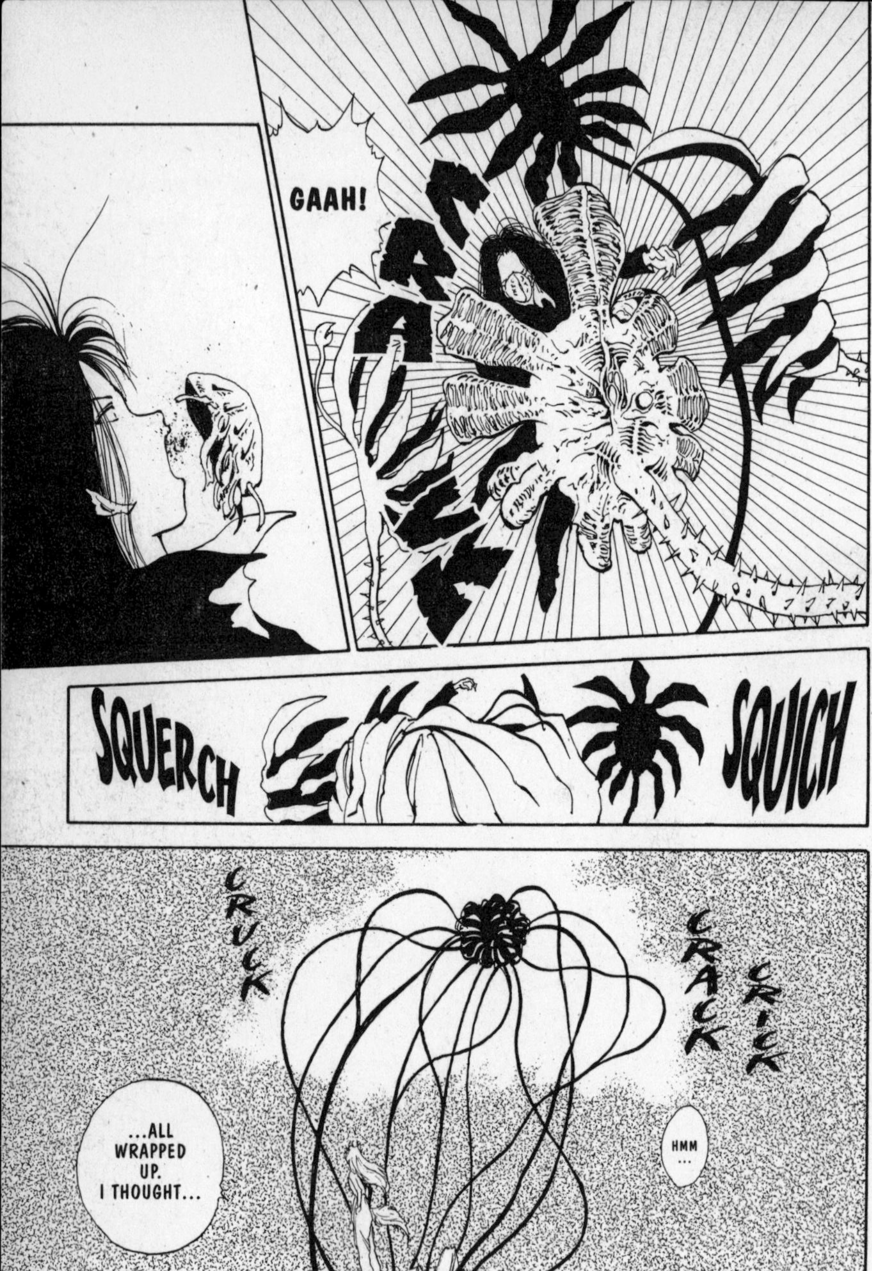
GAAH!
SQUICH
SQUERCH
CRICK
CRACK
HMM ...
CRUCK
...ALL WRAPPED UP. I THOUGHT...

BRR UMM
!
KARASU'S HAIR HAS CHANGED COLOR!
EVEN FROM HERE I CAN SEE HIS AURA BUILDING IN STRENGTH!!
HE'S DRAWING FLAMMABLE ELEMENTS IN...
...TO FUEL A WHOLE-BODY EXPLOSION.
RAAH
HIS HANDS ARE THE FUSES, I BET.
RAAH
BRACE FOR A MAJOR SHOCKWAVE.

HA
HA
HA!
DIE!!
WHAM
LOOKS LIKE A BIG ONE, GUYS.
BETTER GET FURTHER BACK.

READ THIS WAY
!!
KABOOM

HA
HA
HA!
WHOO!
...!!

EVERY-BODY OKAY?!
YAMMER
SEEMS SO...
YATTER
BUT WHERE'S KURAMA?!
HEH...
HUH?!
K-KURAMA?!

YUYU HAKUSHO PUZZLES: ③

EVERYONE IS PLAYING A GAME OF CONCENTRATION.
ANSWER THE TWO QUESTIONS WITH THE
INFORMATION IN THEIR THOUGHTS AS CLUES.

THERE ARE FOUR 3'S LEFT.
EITHER G OR J IS A 6.
I KNOW F ISN'T A MATCH.
THERE ARE FOUR NUMBERS LEFT.
E WAS AN 8.
EITHER G OR H IS A 3.
A AND I ARE THE SAME NUMBER.
B AND I ARE THE SAME NUMBER.
EITHER D OR G IS A 6.
EITHER H OR J IS AN 8.
A
B
C
2
2
D
E
F
G
H
I
J

① WHICH ONE IS THE MATCH FOR C?

② WHAT NUMBER IS F?

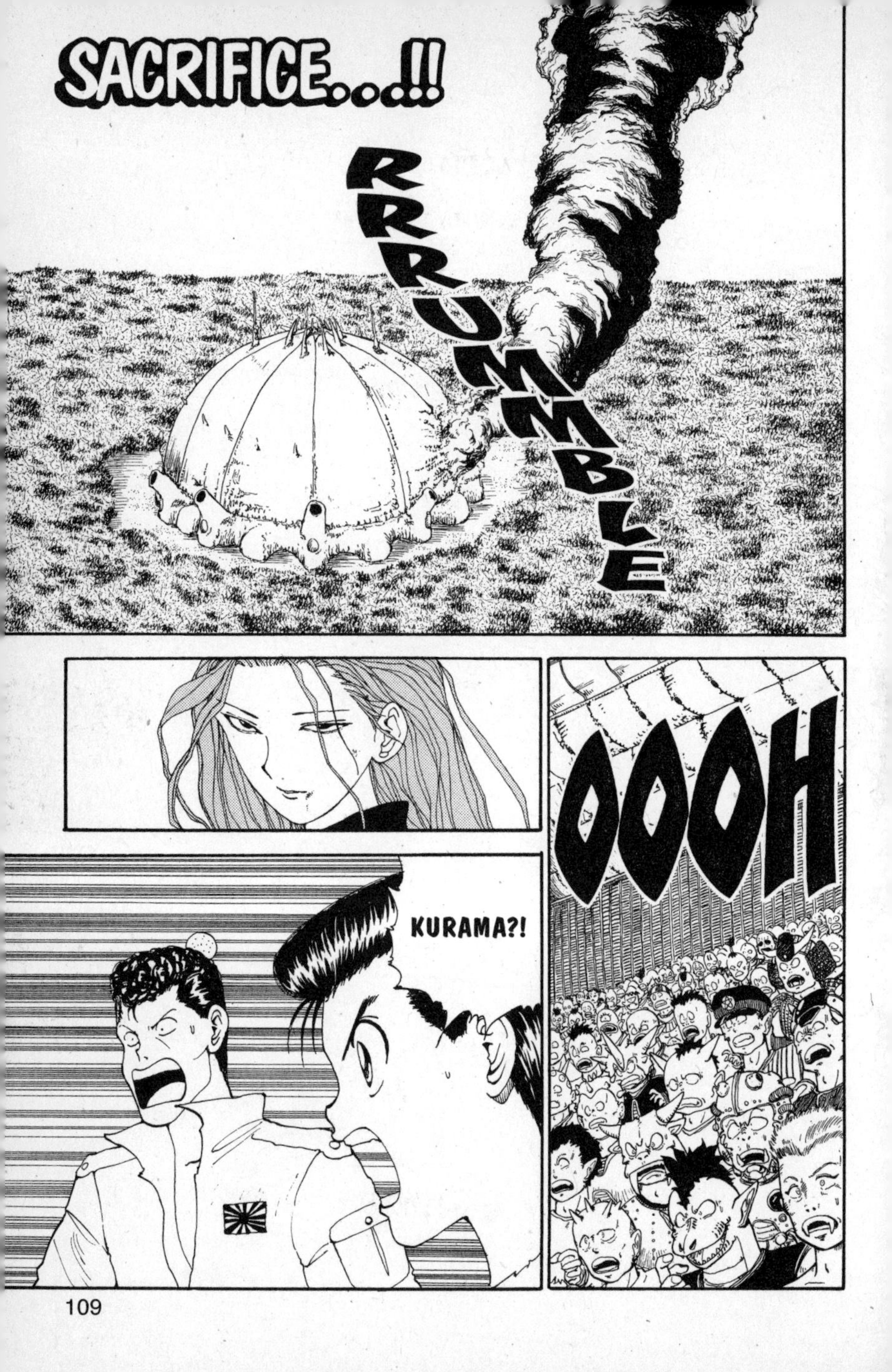
SACRIFICE...!!
RRRUMMBLE
OOOH
KURAMA?!

SACRIFICE...!!

OOOOOOH
KURAMA'S BEEN KNOCKED OUT OF HIS FOX DEMON FORM!!
AND HE LOOKS QUITE A BIT WORSE FOR WEAR!
HE'S CHANGED BACK!
THE POTION MUST'VE WORN OFF!
BUT IT'S ONLY BEEN 5-6 MINUTES!
THE POTION WAS SUPPOSED TO LAST 15!
UNH!
I HAD PLENTY OF TIME LEFT...
...I THOUGHT!
DID ALL THAT PRACTICE CAUSE ME...
...TO BUILD UP RESISTANCE TO THE POTION'S EFFECTS?

SORRY TO INTRUDE ON YOUR THOUGHTS...
...BUT YOU MIGHT WANT TO SAY YOUR PRAYERS.
MAY YOU KNOW A MINIMUM OF PAIN...
RRGH!

READ THIS WAY

?!
YOUR DEMONIC AURA IS TOO WEAK TO ENABLE YOU TO FORM PLANT WEAPONS.
I DARESAY YOU PROBABLY CAN'T EVEN PERCEIVE **MY AURA** AT THIS POINT.
BLAST!
BAM
FWOOSH

!
SCREEEK
WOOSH
FFT!!!
NIP

FWISH
FWISH
FIRST TIME WE'VE EVER SEEN KURAMA FALL BACK ON MARTIAL ARTS!!
KARASU JUST COUNTERS WITH TIGHT, EFFICIENT MOVES!!
KURAMA'S UP TO SOME-THING.
IS PAIN FOGGING YOUR BRAIN?
CLOSING IN ON ME IS SUICIDE!

?!
AS I CAN'T SEE YOUR AURA, PROXIMITY HARDLY MATTERS.
KWAM
SKIIIKKKKK!!

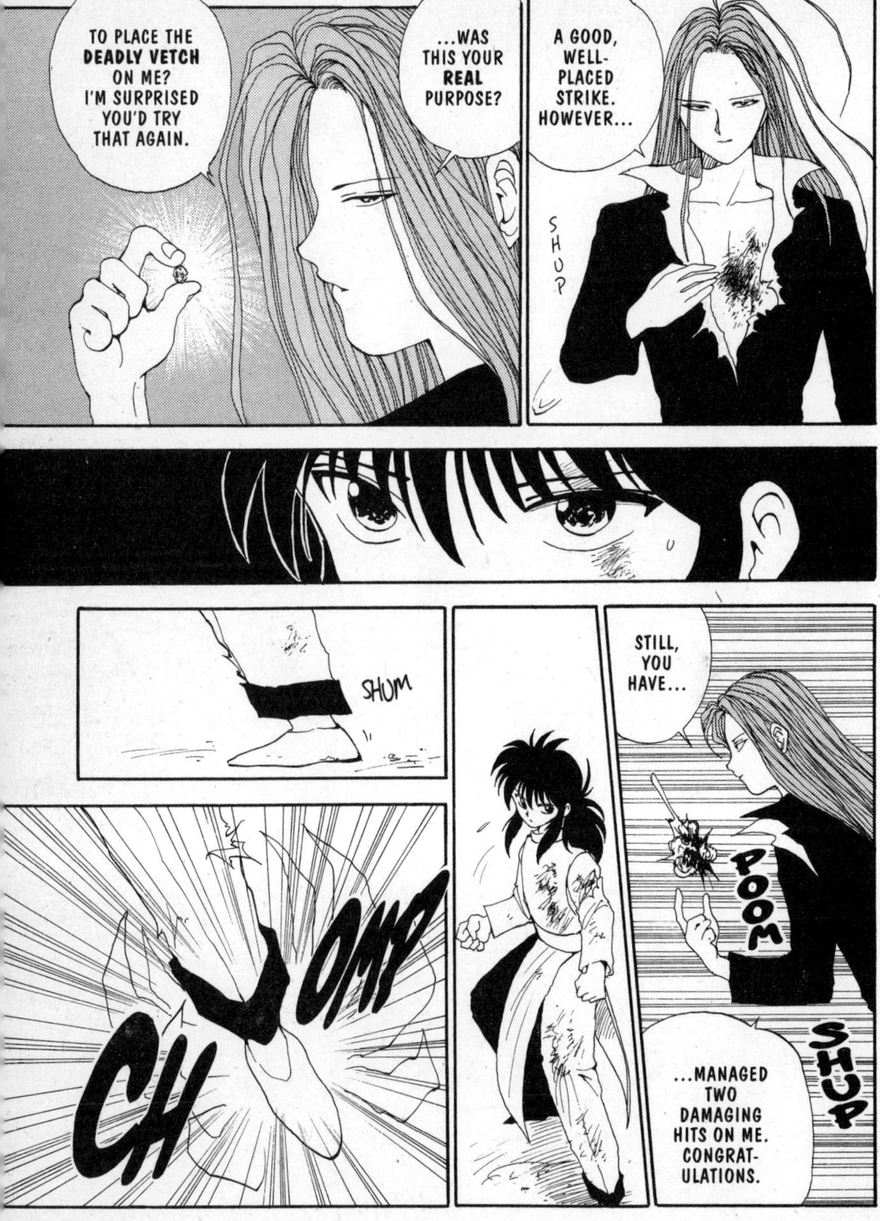
A GOOD, WELL-PLACED STRIKE. HOWEVER...
SHUP
...WAS THIS YOUR REAL PURPOSE?
TO PLACE THE DEADLY VETCH ON ME? I'M SURPRISED YOU'D TRY THAT AGAIN.
STILL, YOU HAVE...
POOM
...MANAGED TWO DAMAGING HITS ON ME. CONGRATULATIONS.
SHUP
SHUM
CHOMP

?!
KRIIIK
GOTCHA.
THAT'S MY "MUDDY BOMB."
BWOOM
AAAGH!
THOOOM

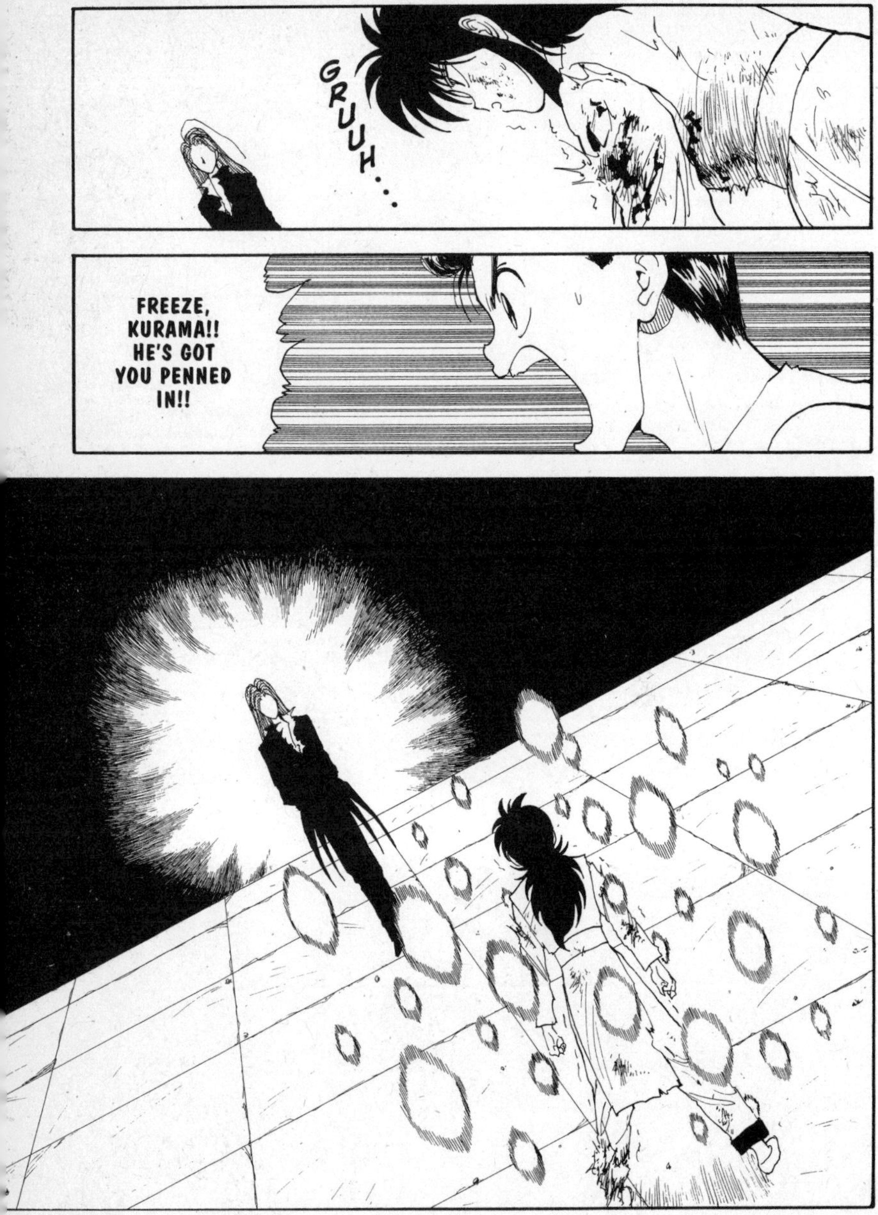
GRUUH...
FREEZE, KURAMA!! HE'S GOT YOU PENNED IN!!

DOES IT MATTER? YOU CAN BARELY STAND.
YOU'RE OUT OF OPTIONS, I'D SAY.
THERE'S NO SUMMONING DEMON PLANE FLORA...
...OR TURNING ORDINARY PLANTS INTO WEAPONS.
I, ON THE OTHER HAND, COULD BLOW YOU TO BITS.
BWAM!
BWOOM!
YAARGH !!

READ THIS WAY

BUT I WON'T. I WISH TO KEEP YOU...
...WITH ME. WELL, YOUR HEAD, AT LEAST.
YOU DON'T SEEM TO HAVE NOTICED...
...THAT MY OPTIONS ARE NOT EXHAUSTED.
YOU SEE, YOU'RE BLEEDING...
...RIGHT OVER YOUR HEART.
THAT'S WHAT MY ATTACK WAS REALLY ABOUT.
RAAH
RAAH
RAAH
RAAH

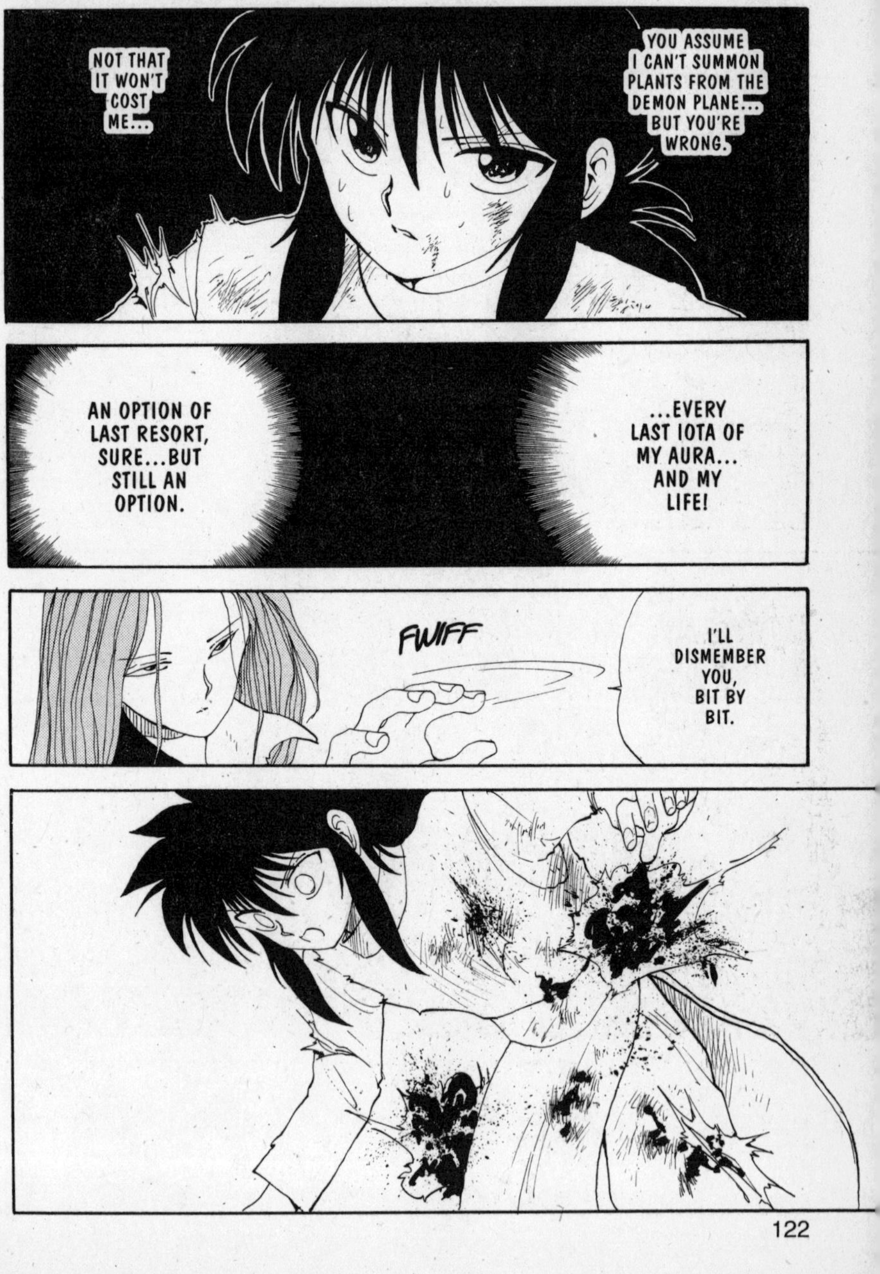
YOU ASSUME I CAN'T SUMMON PLANTS FROM THE DEMON PLANE... BUT YOU'RE WRONG.
NOT THAT IT WON'T COST ME...
...EVERY LAST IOTA OF MY AURA... AND MY LIFE!
AN OPTION OF LAST RESORT, SURE...BUT STILL AN OPTION.
I'LL DISMEMBER YOU, BIT BY BIT.
FWIFF

READ THIS WAY
KURAMA!
THUD
HE'S DOWN!
WOOHOO! THAT'S SWEET, KARASU!
YEEEAH
BOMB 'IM!
BOMB 'IM!
BOMB 'IM!
BOMB 'IM!
BOMB 'IM!
KROOOAR
THE CHEERING'S SO **LOUD** I CAN BARELY THINK!!
FROM WHAT I CAN TELL, THOUGH, JURI'S **TAKING A COUNT!!**

RAAH RAAH
RAAH
RAAH
I SCARCELY THINK THAT'S NECESSARY.
FOR HIM IT'S SIMPLY LIFE...
SWUFF
NO...
...OR DEATH!!
FOR YOU!!
FLASH

READ THIS WAY

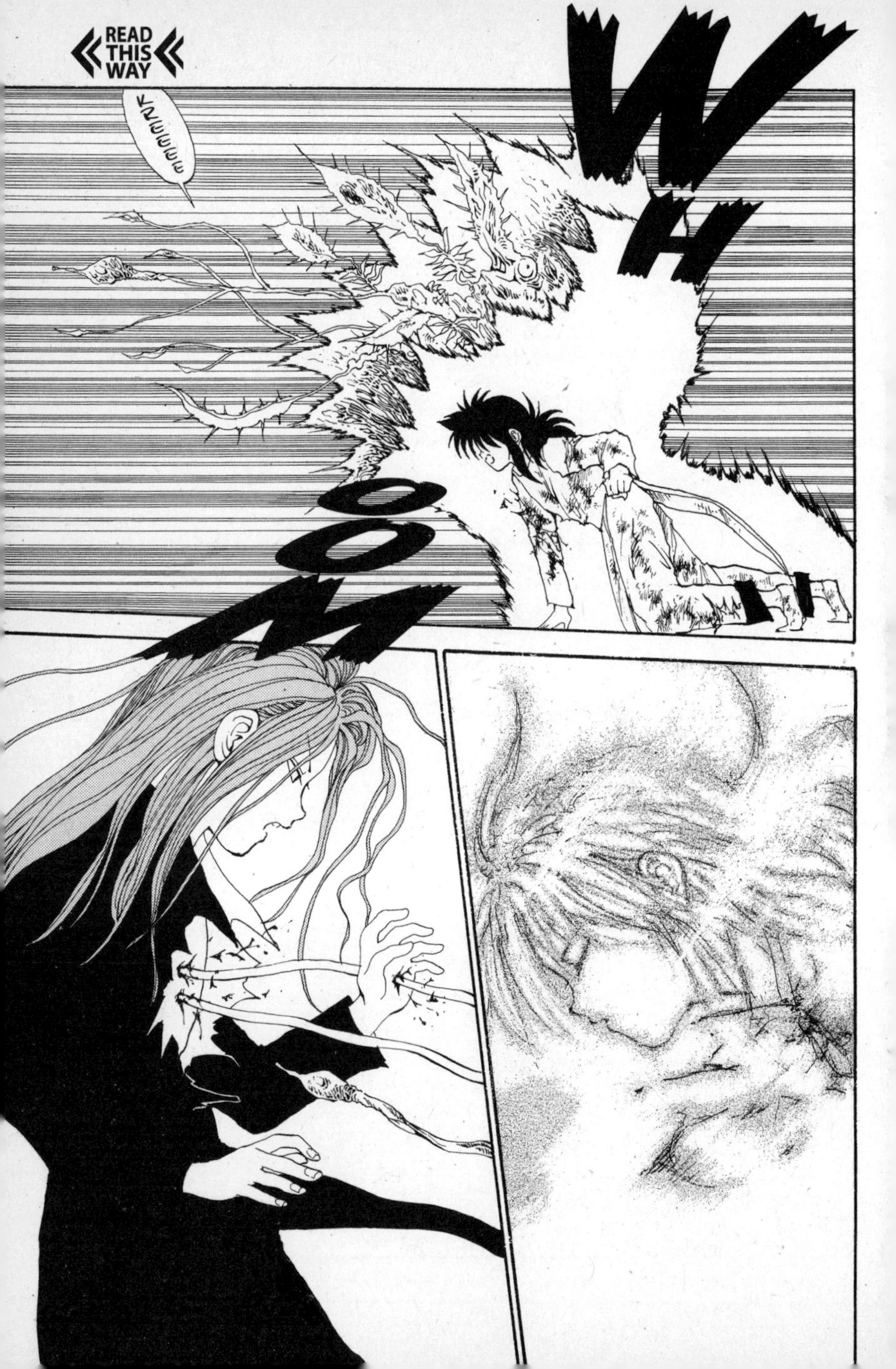

A... VAMPIRE PLANT...?
I DON'T... HE COULDN'T... HAVE SUMMONED...
KURAMA!!
TWITCH
I'M...ALIVE?
HOW...?

READ THIS WAY

DID MY AURA...
...RENEW WITHOUT MY KNOWING?!
THE POTION'S EFFECTS DIDN'T WEAKEN AFTER ALL!!
THE FOX DEMON'S POWERS ARE RETURNING TO SHUICHI MINAMINO'S BODY!!
KURAMA'S WON!!
A MIND-BLOWIN' COMEBACK !!
OOOOH

THE REASON BEHIND THE ARMOR!!
WAY TO GO, KURAMA! YER THE COMEBACK KID!!
RAAH
ONE DOWN, TWO TO GO!!
RAAH
LEMME HELP YA, KURAMA!
THANKS. SORRY ABOUT THE MATCH.
HUH?
AND THE WINNER...
...OF THIS MATCH: KARASU!!
HEH ...

THE REASON BEHIND THE ARMOR!!

GOING INTO THE NEXT MATCH...THESE GUYS!!

BUI

VS

HIEI

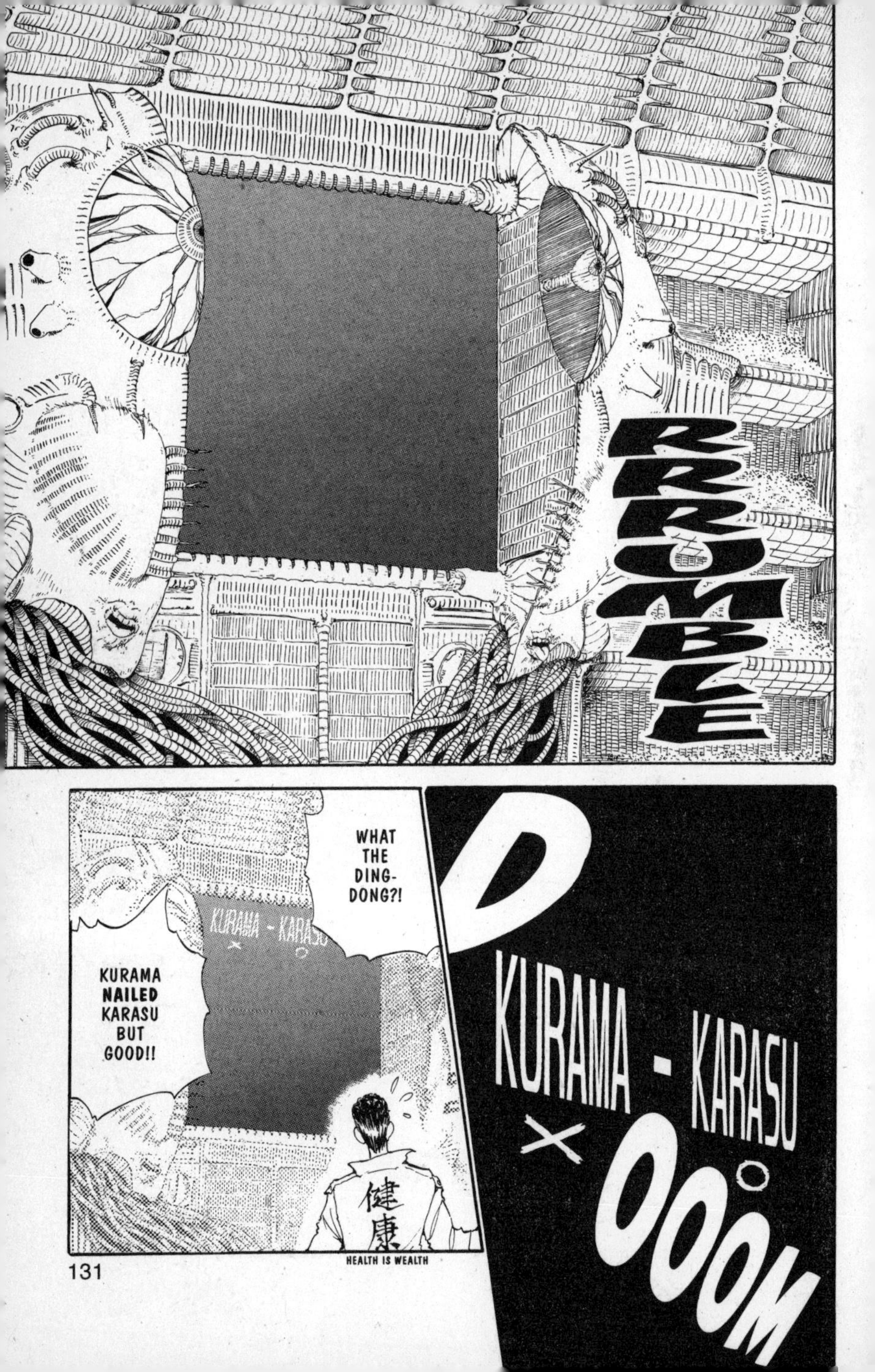
RRUMBLE
DOOOM
KURAMA - KARASU
× ○
WHAT THE DING-DONG?!
KURAMA NAILED KARASU BUT GOOD!!
KURAMA - KARASU
× ○
健康
HEALTH IS WEALTH

KURAMA TOOK THE FULL COUNT!
I DO MY JOB, Y'KNOW.
HE STRUCK BACK WHILE STILL TECHNICALLY DOWN!
AND WAS NOT BACK UP UNTIL AFTER I COUNTED TO 10!
OOOH
10 COUNTS...?!
I COULDN'T HEAR...
HARDLY ANYONE COULD.
WE DIDN'T HEAR JURI'S COUNT OVER ALL THE WILD CHEERING!!
INSTANT REPLAY CONFIRMS KURAMA WAS NOT UP BEFORE THE COUNT WAS COMPLETE!
YEAH! TAKE THAT, TEAM URAMESHI!
TEAM TOGURO WILL GETCHA IN TWO!

GETCHA IN TWO!
GETCHA IN TWO!
GETCHA IN TWO!
BOO BOO
DIE!
KUWABARA!
SHUT UP! WE MAY'VE LOST THE MATCH, BUT WE WON THE FIGHT!
YOU SHUT UP!
GRRR
GRARR
DROP DEAD!
HE WHO LIVES LONGEST, LAUGHS LAST!!
HUUUSH...
I WOULDN'T COUNT ON THAT.
DON'T FORGET, EACH WINNING TEAM MEMBER GETS HIS HEART'S DESIRE.
YOU KNOW WHAT I DESIRE?
OH SURE, THEY SHUT UP FOR HIM!
TO SEE YOU DEAD... EVERY ONE OF YOU.

KILL!
KILL!
KILL!
GRRR!
MY HEART'S DESIRE IS TO NEVER...
...ATTEND ANOTHER OF THESE ASININE TOURNAMENTS.
I WISH ITS BACKERS WOULD ALL DROP DEAD.
RAAH
RAAH
YUSUKE ...
...I WANTED TO FIGHT "SHADES" TOGURO...
...BUT I'LL YIELD TO YOU FOR GENKAI'S SAKE.
HIEI ...

I'LL MAKE DO WITH "MR. AXE."

RAAAAH
WHACK THAT RUNT IN TWO!!
YEAH! GET 'IM, BUI!!
THINK I'M HEIGHT CHALLENGED, EH?
HUH! THEY'RE CURSE BINDINGS!
HE SKIPPED SOME BASIC STEPS, THOUGH.
HASN'T THAT ARM HEALED?
YOW!! HE'S GOT BANDAGES ON BANDAGES NOW!
WHAT'RE THOSE?
DID HE REALLY MANAGE IT...SO QUICKLY?

DID HE MASTER THE BLACK DRAGON?!
BEGIN!!
DASH

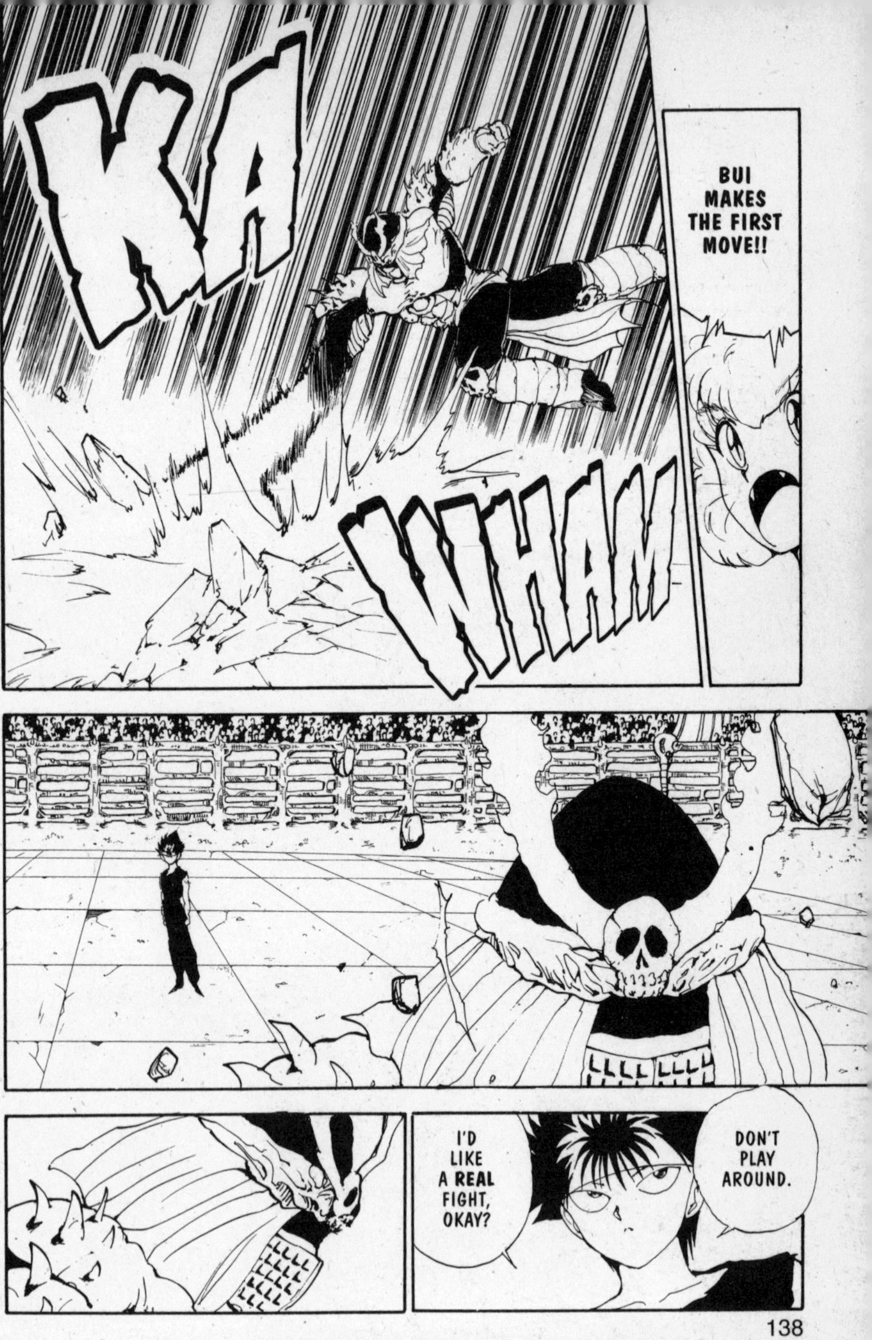
BUI MAKES THE FIRST MOVE!!
KA
WHAM
DON'T PLAY AROUND.
I'D LIKE A REAL FIGHT, OKAY?

CLENCH
CR
ACK
FLING
HOLY...
... WHAT STRENGTH !!

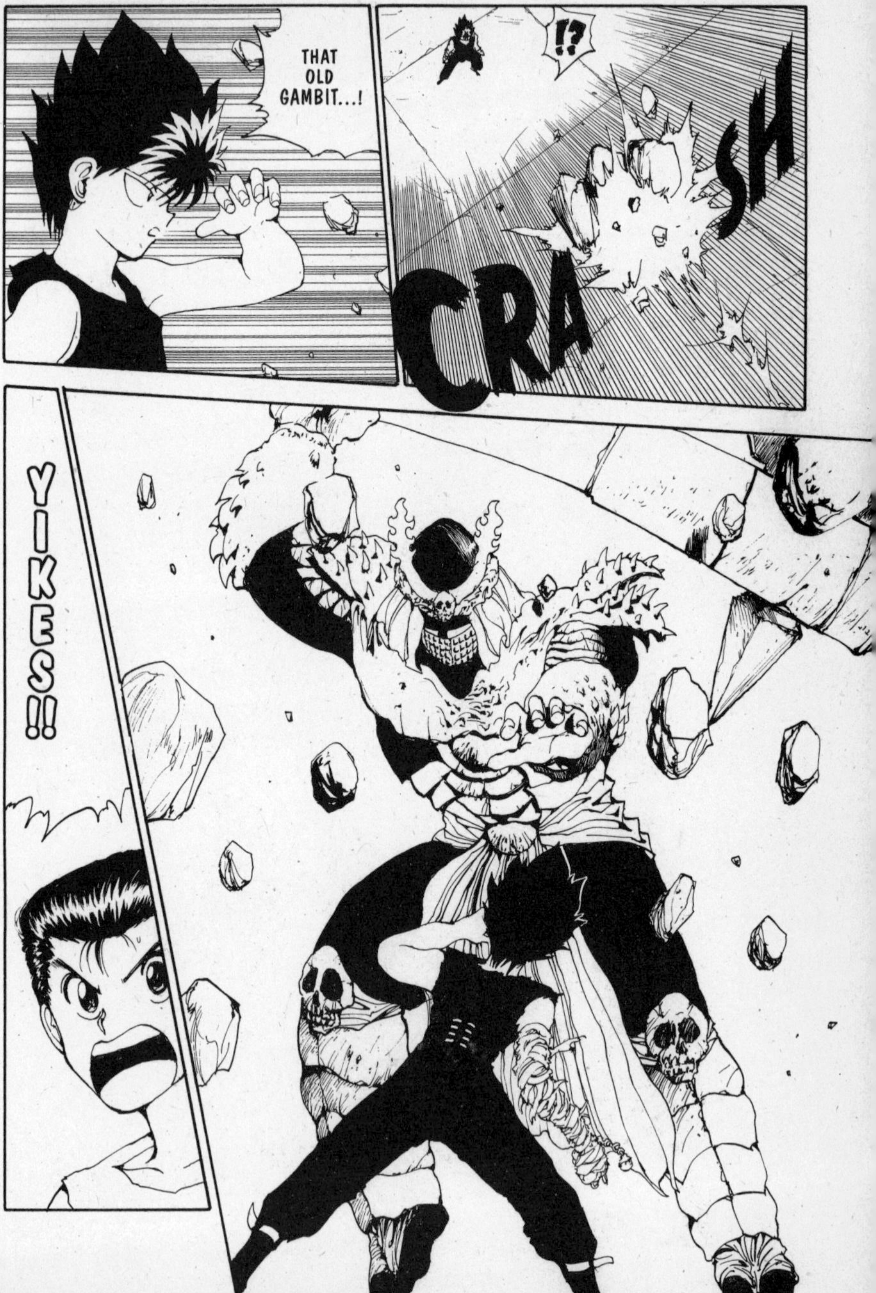
!?
CRASH
THAT OLD GAMBIT...!
YIKES!!

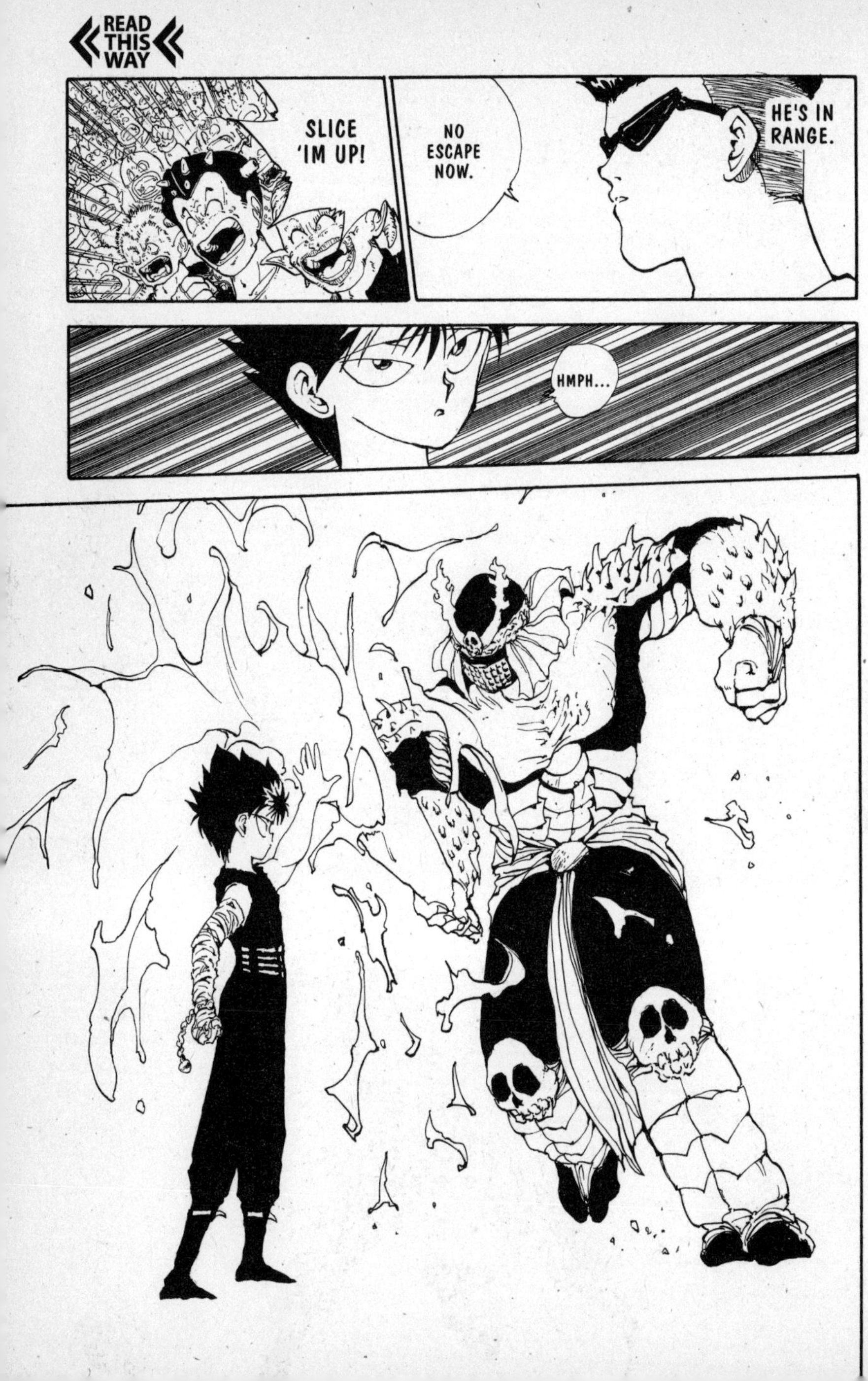
READ THIS WAY
HE'S IN RANGE.
NO ESCAPE NOW.
SLICE 'IM UP!
HMPH...

!?
!!
LIKE I SAID... DON'T PLAY AROUND.
DID YOU THINK AN AURA-LESS SCRAP OF IRON WOULD BOTHER ME?
I'M GIVING SERIOUS THOUGHT TO BEING INSULTED.
H-HE MELTED THAT HUGE AXE LIKE IT WAS A CHOCOLATE BAR!
NO QUESTION HIEI'S GAINED...
...A NEW LEVEL OF POWER!

READ THIS WAY
YOU HAVE CONVINCED ME THAT...
...THIS ARMOR WON'T DO ME ANY GOOD AT ALL.
WOW! DIDYA HEAR THAT, TOURNAMENT FANS?
FOR THE VERY FIRST TIME, BUI SPOKE! WHAT A DEEP VOICE HE'S GOT!
CHINK
FLING
THWOOOM
WOOOOW
YOW! THAT GUY WAS WEARING ENOUGH ARMOR FOR A TANK!
THWOOSH THWOOSH
HEY, KID WITH THE SPIKY HAIR! HE'S OPEN! HIT 'IM!!
SHUSH! I DON'T THINK THAT'S HIS STYLE.
ARMOR NORMALLY PROTECTS THE BODY FROM ATTACK.
BUT IN MY CASE...

...IT SERVES AS A RESTRAINT.
YOU SEE, MY POWERS AREN'T EASY TO CONTAIN.
HEY, THIS SOUNDS PROMISING!
BUT NOT FOR YOU, YOU SMUG LITTLE RUNT!

WHOOOSH
A BATTLE AURA! THAT'S WHAT **REALLY** PROTECTS HIM!
BIGGEST I'VE SEEN... EVEN ALLOWS HIM TO **LEVITATE!**
HOPE YOU MEANT WHAT YOU SAID.
I, TOO, WANT A **MEMORABLE** MATCH.

OH, IT WILL BE.
LOOP
LOOP
HE'S REMOVING THOSE BANDAGES!
WHAT ARE CURSE BINDINGS, ANYWAY?!
JUST LIKE BUI'S ARMOR... THEY'RE TALISMANS, TO RESTRAIN HIS POWER...
...BECAUSE ONCE SET LOOSE, SUCH POWER IS UNSTOPPABLE.
WHEN THOSE TWO POWERS CLASH...
THIS STADIUM WILL BE TORN APART!!

READ THIS WAY

HM?!
I DON'T REMEMBER HOW THESE...
...GO BACK ON, SO THERE'S NO GOING BACK NOW.

PLAY FAIR! PEEK ONLY IF YOU'RE REALLY STUCK!
DON'T SWEAT IT IF YOU COULDN'T SOLVE THE PUZZLES!!
LET'S GO!!
THE ANSWERS ARE ON P.168!

WATCH HOW I'VE MASTERED THE BLACK DRAGON!!
EAT OR BE EATEN!!
TH-THE BLACK DRAGON...?!
HIEI'S UNVEILED ONE HECK OF AN AURA!!

C'MON!
EAT OR BE EATEN!!
THE BLACK DRAGON! THE ULTIMATE TECHNIQUE OF THE BLAZING FIST OF THE OVERLORD.
IF I CAN WARD IT OFF, I'LL WIN!!

READ THIS WAY

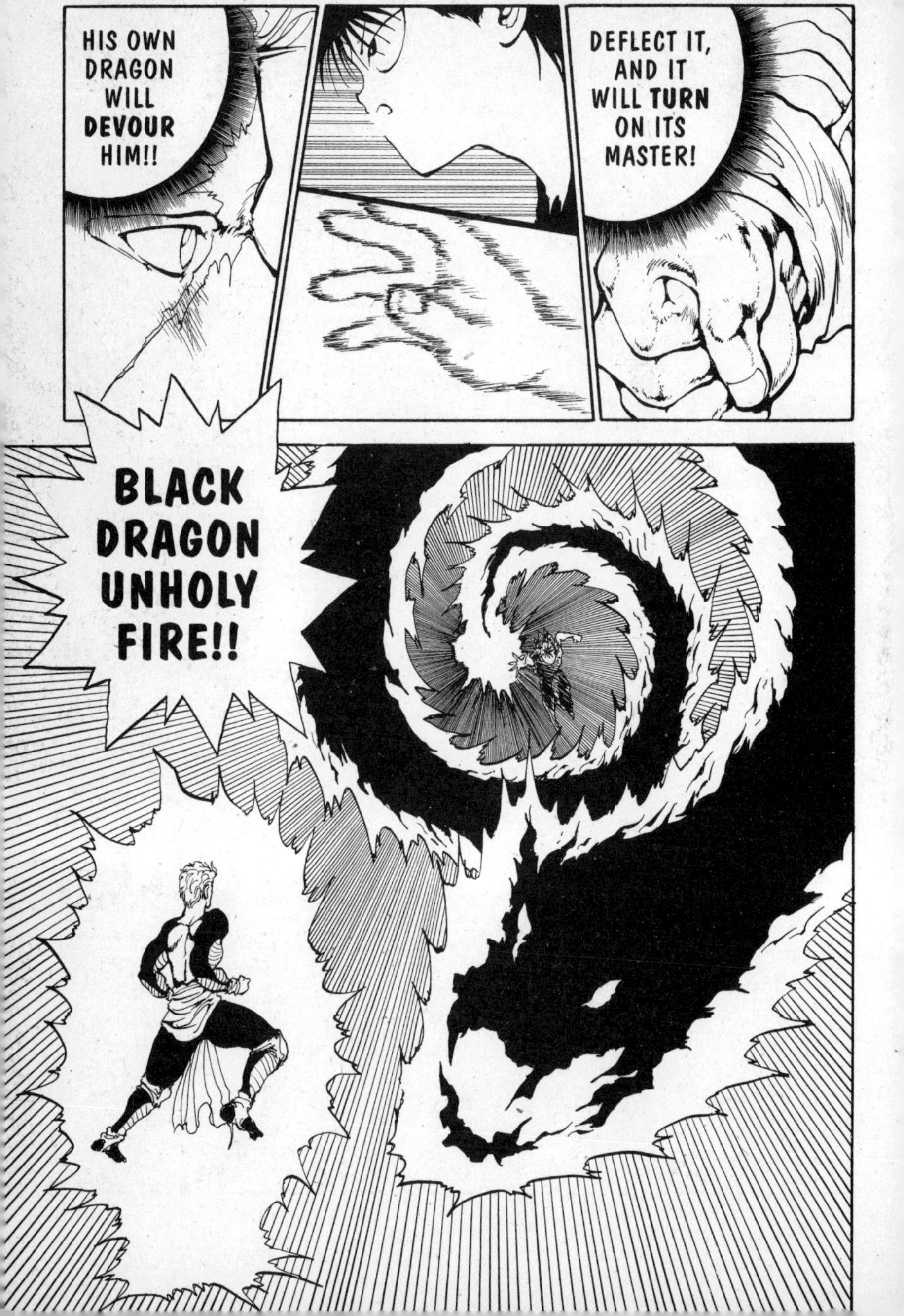
DEFLECT IT, AND IT WILL TURN ON ITS MASTER!
HIS OWN DRAGON WILL DEVOUR HIM!!
BLACK DRAGON UNHOLY FIRE!!

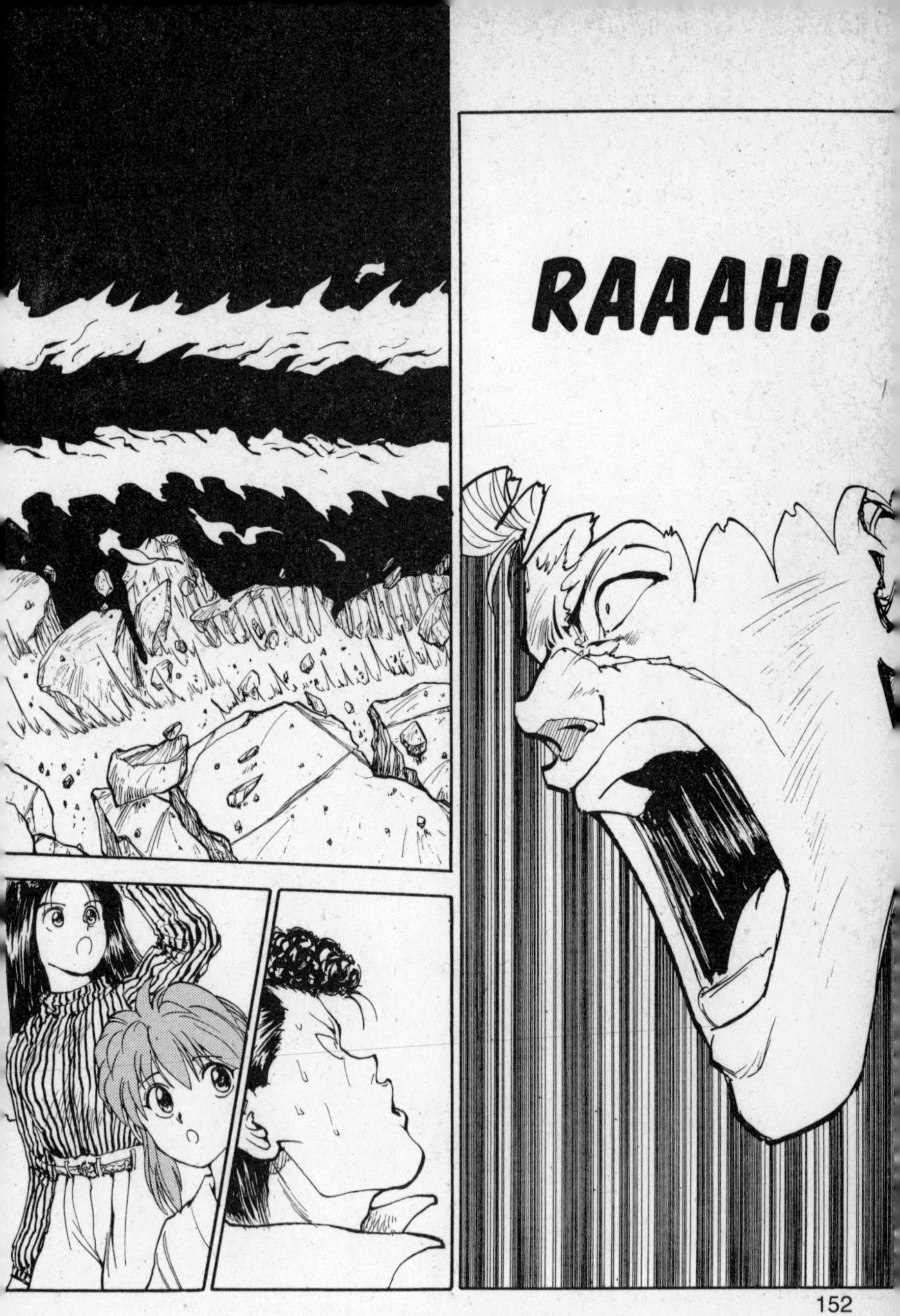
RAAAH!

BOOSTER ROCKET BUTTON
AT THE READY.

NARRR!
FWWW
BAWHOOOM
...
WHAM
TH-THE BLACK DRAGON'S LOOSE AND RUNNING AMOK!!
WEAKER SPECTATORS ARE BEING INCINERATED!!

RAA-
AH!
HRRRUNN
DID
IT!!

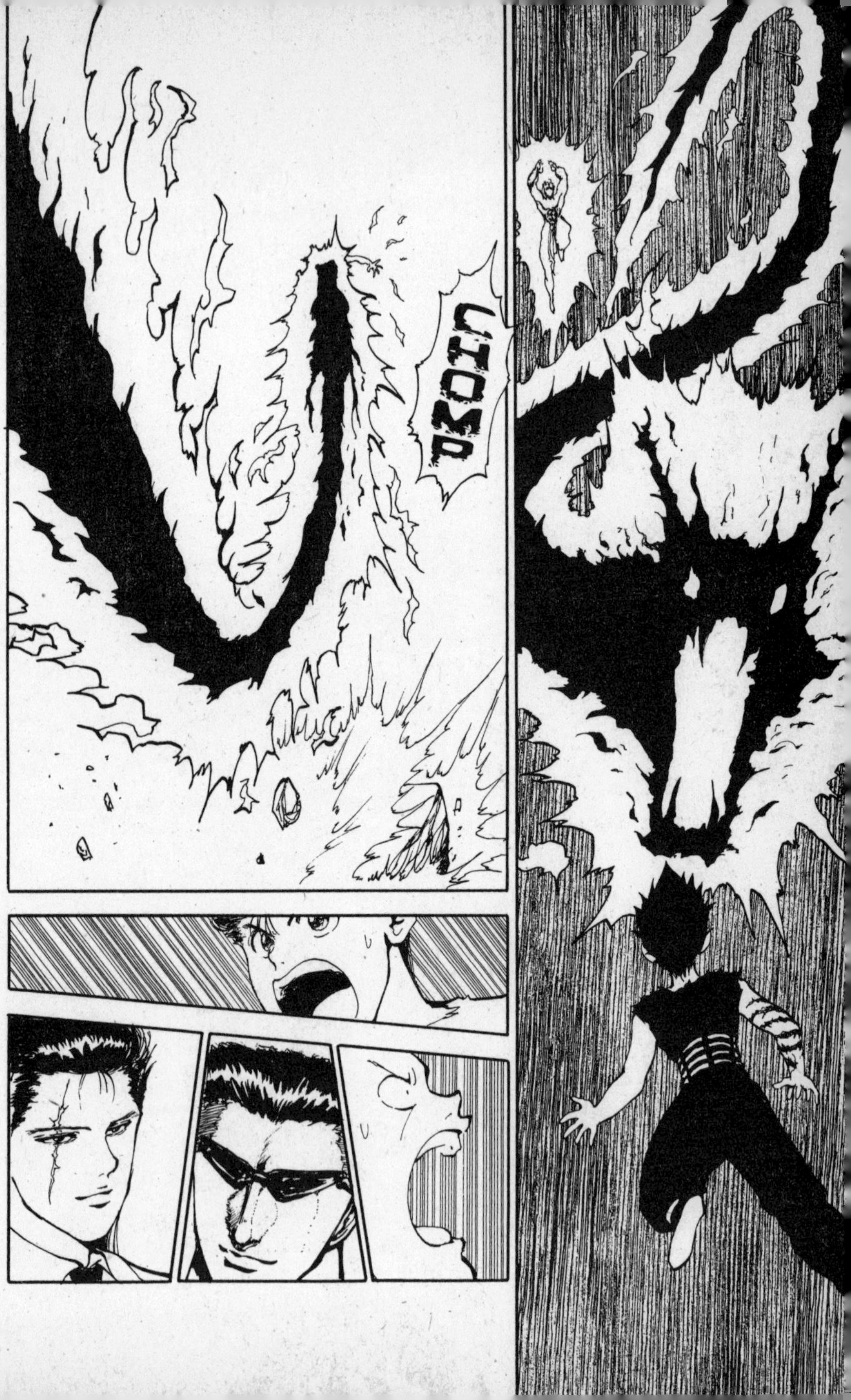
CHOMP

TUMP
HA HAAH!! THAT'S THE MATCH!!
I'VE DEFEATED THE BLAZING FIST!!
THAT'S TWO WINS IN A ROW FOR TEAM TOGURO!!
WAAAHOO
STADIUM'S A SHAMBLES, THOUGH.
HE...
...HE BEAT HIEI...

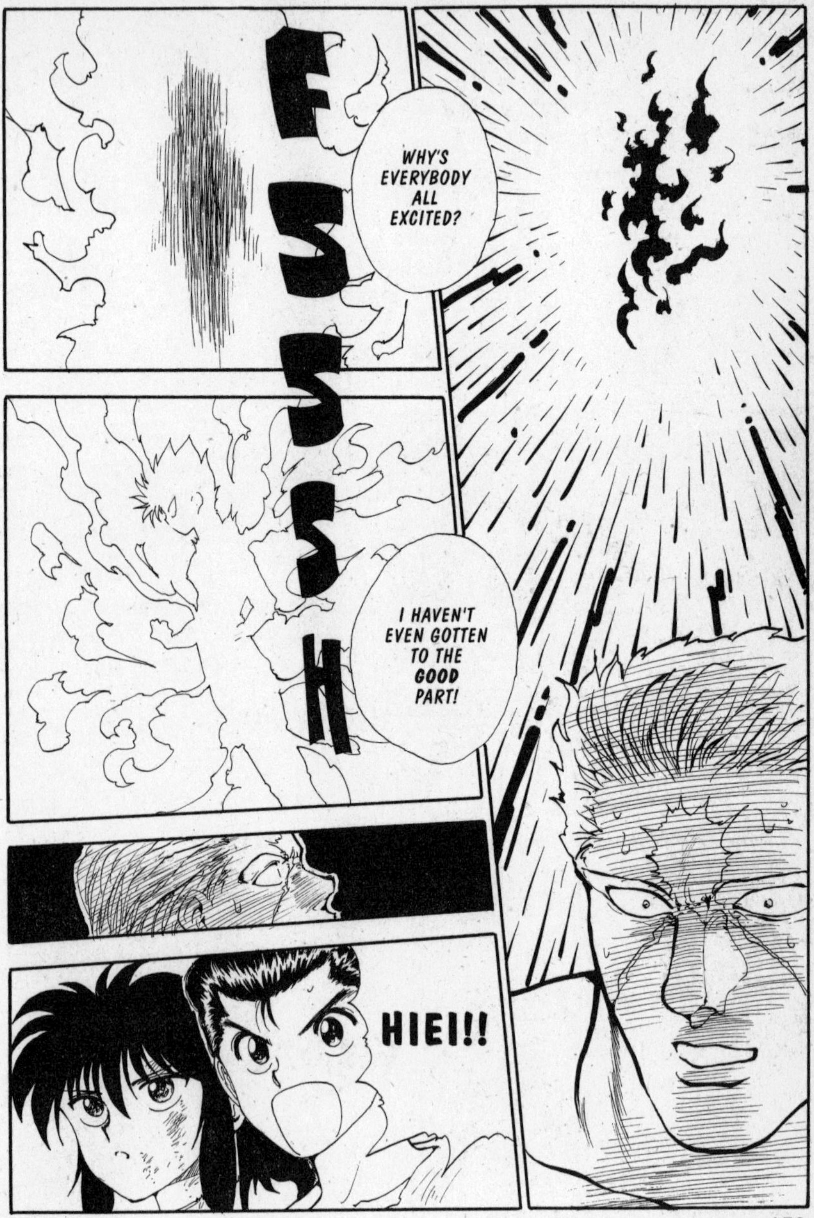

FSSSSH
WHY'S EVERYBODY ALL EXCITED?
I HAVEN'T EVEN GOTTEN TO THE GOOD PART!
HIEI!!

READ THIS WAY

WHAT? HOW?
BUZZZ
BUZZZ
HE SEEMS THE SAME... THOSE MARKS ON HIS ARM ARE GONE, THOUGH.
DON'T JUST STAND THERE, BUI! SMASH 'IM!!
SO THAT'S WHAT HE MEANT...
YES ...
...HE CONSUMED THE BLACK DRAGON!!
A TRUE MASTER CAN ATTAIN DOMINANCE OVER AND ABSORB THE BLACK DRAGON'S IMMENSE ENERGY.
BUI'S SUFFICIENTLY ADVANCED TO KNOW WHAT HE'S NOW UP AGAINST.
UNH...!!
SEE IT?
YES, YOU RECOGNIZE A TRUE MASTERY OF THE BLACK DRAGON.

IT'S NOT A WEAPON, NOT IN THE WAY MOST MIGHT EXPECT.
WHAT IT DOES IS **ENHANCE** ITS MASTER'S CAPACITIES TO THE **NTH DEGREE!**

READ THIS WAY
BLAST YOU!!
ARR...!
KWAM
KWAM
YAAH!

WHAM
RRR...
HURK!

FFFT
PWAM
WHOOMP
KA-

TUMP
DO IT...
...FINISH ME. WHEN TOGURO FIRST DEFEATED ME...I KNEW I COULD IMPROVE, GET STRONGER.
THE PROSPECT OF A REMATCH MOTIVATED ME TO EXCEED MYSELF, BUT...
...TOGURO IMPROVED, TOO.
SO MUCH SO, I'VE **NO HOPE** OF CHALLENGING HIM AGAIN.
LOSING TO YOU CONFIRMS IT.
I'VE NO REASON LEFT TO LIVE.
HMPH!
YOU WANT TO DIE, DO IT **YOURSELF.**

8!
9!
TWUNG
I DON'T TAKE ORDERS FROM NOBODY!
10!! THE MATCH IS OVER!!
THE WINNER: HIEI!

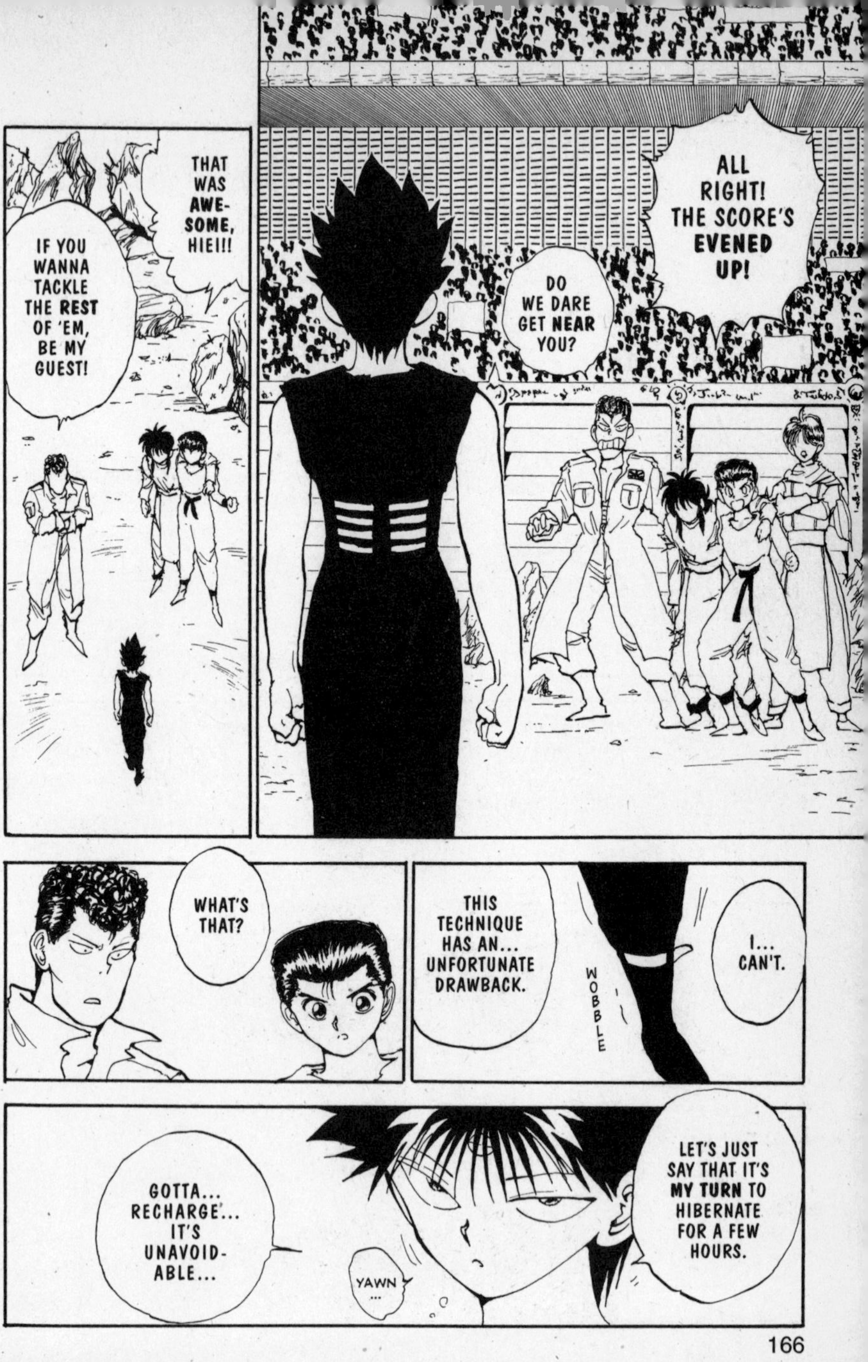
ALL RIGHT! THE SCORE'S EVENED UP!
DO WE DARE GET NEAR YOU?
THAT WAS AWE-SOME, HIEI!!!
IF YOU WANNA TACKLE THE REST OF 'EM, BE MY GUEST!
I... CAN'T.
WOBBLE
THIS TECHNIQUE HAS AN... UNFORTUNATE DRAWBACK.
WHAT'S THAT?
LET'S JUST SAY THAT IT'S MY TURN TO HIBERNATE FOR A FEW HOURS.
YAWN ...
GOTTA... RECHARGE... IT'S UNAVOIDABLE...

...BUT...
...I'LL TRUST YOU SORRY WIMPS...TO HOLD UP... OUR SIDE.
IF... WHEN I WAKE UP... I FIND YOU'VE LOST...
...YOU'LL BE... BE...
... SORRY...!
THWUMP
...
. . .
HUH...?...... . . .
PFFT!
ARROGANT AND OVER-BEARING TO THE LAST.
HMM...
GOTTA SAY...
...HE LOOKS SO PEACEFUL...
...YOU WOULDN'T THINK HE'D JUST BLOWN THIS STADIUM APART.
SNORE
I COULD GRAFFITI HIS FACE...

POOT
HEH HEH I'M NOT TELLIN'! YOU CAN KISS MY BUTT!

THE ANSWERS WILL BE IN VOL. 12!
WAY TOO RUDE!!

KUWABARA SNAPS!!

AH! YOU'RE AWAKE.
...
SO... HOW LONG WAS I OUT?!
ABOUT SIX HOURS.
AND THE TOURNAMENT? HOW'S IT GOING?
AFTER YOUR WIN, THEY CALLED A HALT.
HUH? WHY?

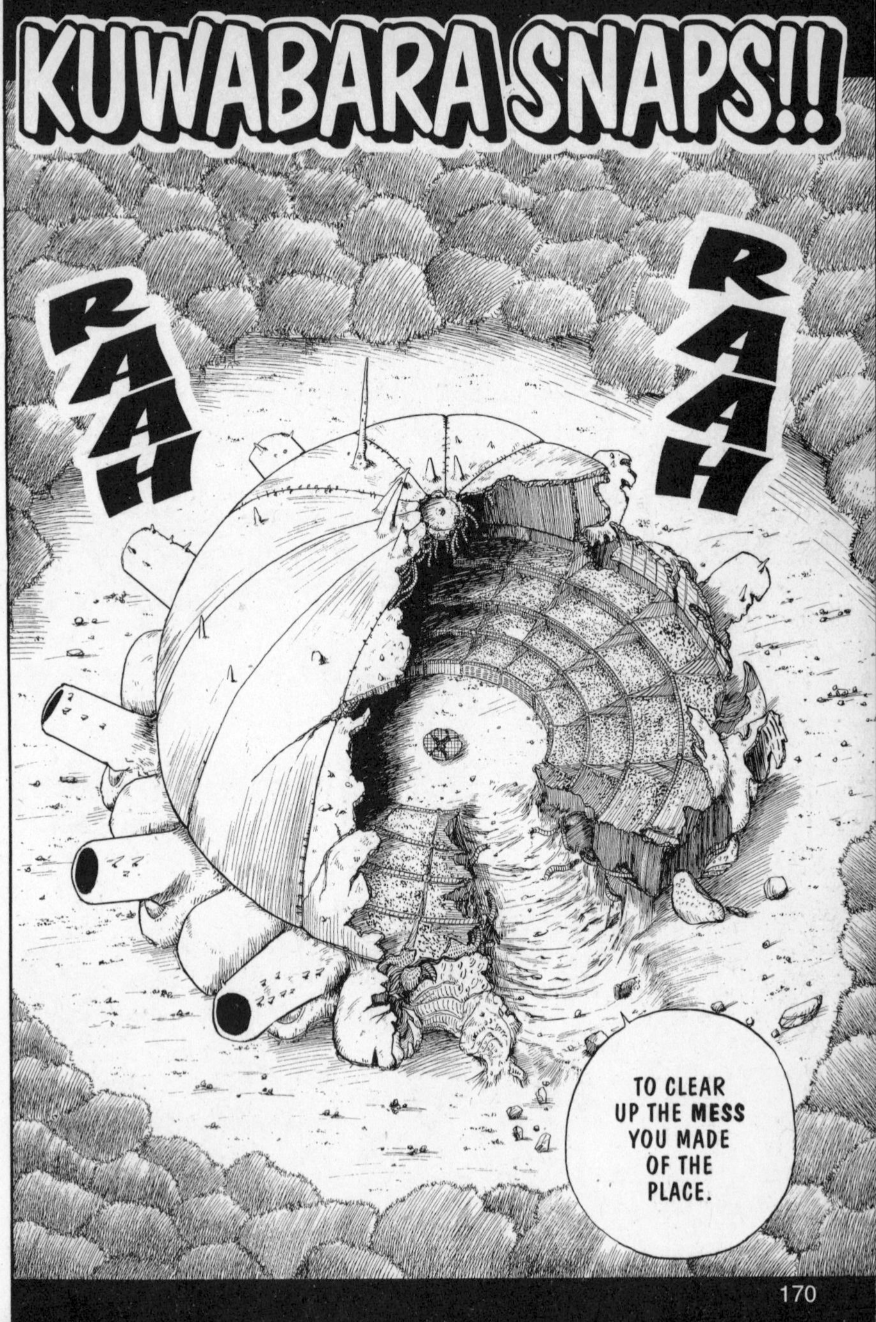
KUWABARA SNAPS!!
RAAH
RAAH
TO CLEAR UP THE MESS YOU MADE OF THE PLACE.

READ THIS WAY
SORRY FOR THE WAIT, FOLKS! BUT NOW WE'RE READY TO GO!
LET'S HAVE THE THIRD MATCH!
WE'RE UNDER WAY AGAIN AFTER A SIX-HOUR BREAK!!
ALL RIIIGHT!
NUTHIN'LL STOP THE TOGUROS NOW!
WHICH HASN'T DAMPENED THE ENTHUSIASM OF THIS CROWD!!
I'M UP NEXT!
RAAH
RAAH
RAAH
DIE!
RAAH
THEN COME UP AND DIE, HUMAN!
DIE!

STILL FAVORING THE TOGUROS?
EVEN AFTER I DEFEATED BUI AND KNOCKED 'EM AROUND LIKE THAT?
WHILE YOU WERE ASLEEP...
...TOGURO IMPRESSED THEM WITH A LITTLE STUNT.
HE HAULED OVER THE RING FROM THE OLD ARENA?!
TO SALUTE YOUR SPECTACULAR EFFORT, HE SAID.

READ THIS WAY
WE'RE RIGHT BACK IN THE CROWD'S BAD BOOKS.
HE REMINDED 'EM WHAT A MONSTER HE IS!
WELL, SO WHAT!! I HAVE MY SUPER SPECIAL SWORD!!
YOU OKAY? BOWELS ACTING UP, PERHAPS?
I'M FINE, THANKS!
WHAT USE ARE YOU, ANYWAY?
IF GENKAI WERE HERE, I COULD'VE TACKLED THE MIDDLE-AGED DUDE.
HE STILL DOESN'T KNOW SHE'S DEAD?
THAT'S WHAT IT LOOKS LIKE...
YUSUKE ...
...WHY HAVEN'T YOU TOLD HIM?
SHOULD'VE TOLD HIM MYSELF.

RAAH
DIE!
RAAH
TUMP
DIE!
RAAH
I'LL MAKE THE FIRST STRIKE!!
THAT'LL SHUT 'EM UP FOR A WHILE!!
BEGIN!!
GRR!

READ THIS WAY
HUH?!
MY, MY...
HIS RECUPERATIVE POWERS HAVE BEEN BOOSTED.
THE SWORD'S AURA IS ALSO ENHANCED. IT'S BOTH A WEAPON AND A SHIELD.
HAVE AT YOU!!

DASH
THAT SWORD'S NO TOY.
SO... MAYBE I'LL TRY...
CRACK
?!
THOSE CRACKS...!!
RAAH!

READ THIS WAY
WHY'S HE JUST STANDING THERE?!
?!
THWUNK
SKLOOP

EH?
IS... IS THAT IT?
...
D-DID I...
...DID I ACTUALLY WIN?
TH...
SHUNK

KUWABARA !!
THUD
CRUNK

UNH ...
健康第一
HEH HEH HEH...
SUCH NAIVETÉ... IT'S QUITE ENTERTAINING, REALLY.
CRICK
CRUNCH
HOLY...
...SPIT! TWO OF HIM!!
CRUCKLE
CRACK
YOU ATTACKED AN EXTRUDED MANNEQUIN.
IT FEELS PAIN, BUT YOU FEEL IT WORSE.
POP

SWIRL TWIRL
MY ORGANS ARE ALL RATHER FREE-FLOATING.
CRUGGLE
I DRILLED THROUGH THE STONE WITH MY FEET... THAT'S HOW I GOT OVER HERE.
A MEMENTO FROM GENKAI?
A HANDY, WELL-MADE DEVICE.
?!
HOW CAN SHE HOPE TO REST IN PEACE?
FUNNY... SUCH A GIFT, WASTED ON SUCH A NITWIT.
YOU MEAN... YOU DIDN'T **KNOW?**
THIS **SURPRISES** YOU?
DID YOU JUST **SAY—?**
WHAT?
GENKAI IS **DEAD.**
KILLED IN A FIGHT.

WHAT...?
BUT...
GENKAI...
...WON'T BE WITH US TODAY.
SHEE... HOW NAÏVE CAN YOU GET?
WHAT'D YOU SAY?!
Y'MEAN I'M THE ONLY ONE...
...WHO DIDN'T KNOW?
UNH!
HEH HEH HEH HEH...
HEH HEH HEH...

YOUR "FRIENDS" DIDN'T BOTHER TO INFORM YOU?
HA HA HA HA HA HA!
I'LL TELL YOU THE TALE...
CRICKLE
CRUCKLE
...WITH A LITTLE PUPPET SHOW.
DOOM
!
ONCE, LONG AGO, TWO DEAR FRIENDS...
...A YOUNG MAN AND WOMAN, TOGETHER SOUGHT TO MASTER THE MARTIAL ARTS.
BUT TIME PASSED... THE WOMAN AGED, LOST HER LOOKS...
ZWOOP
CONSUMED BY JEALOUSY, THE WOMAN CHALLENGED HIM TO A DUEL.
BROTHER!
THIS WON'T TAKE LONG.
THE MAN, THOUGH, CALLED ON THE POWERS OF THE DEMON PLANE TO PRESERVE HIS YOUTH.
SADLY, SHE WAS OFF HER GAME... BUT HE WASN'T.

THOONK!
AND SO MY BROTHER FINISHED IT...
...LIKE THIS... AND SHE WENT TO HEAVEN.
AND HE LIVED HAPPILY EVER AFTER.
HA HA HA HA HA!

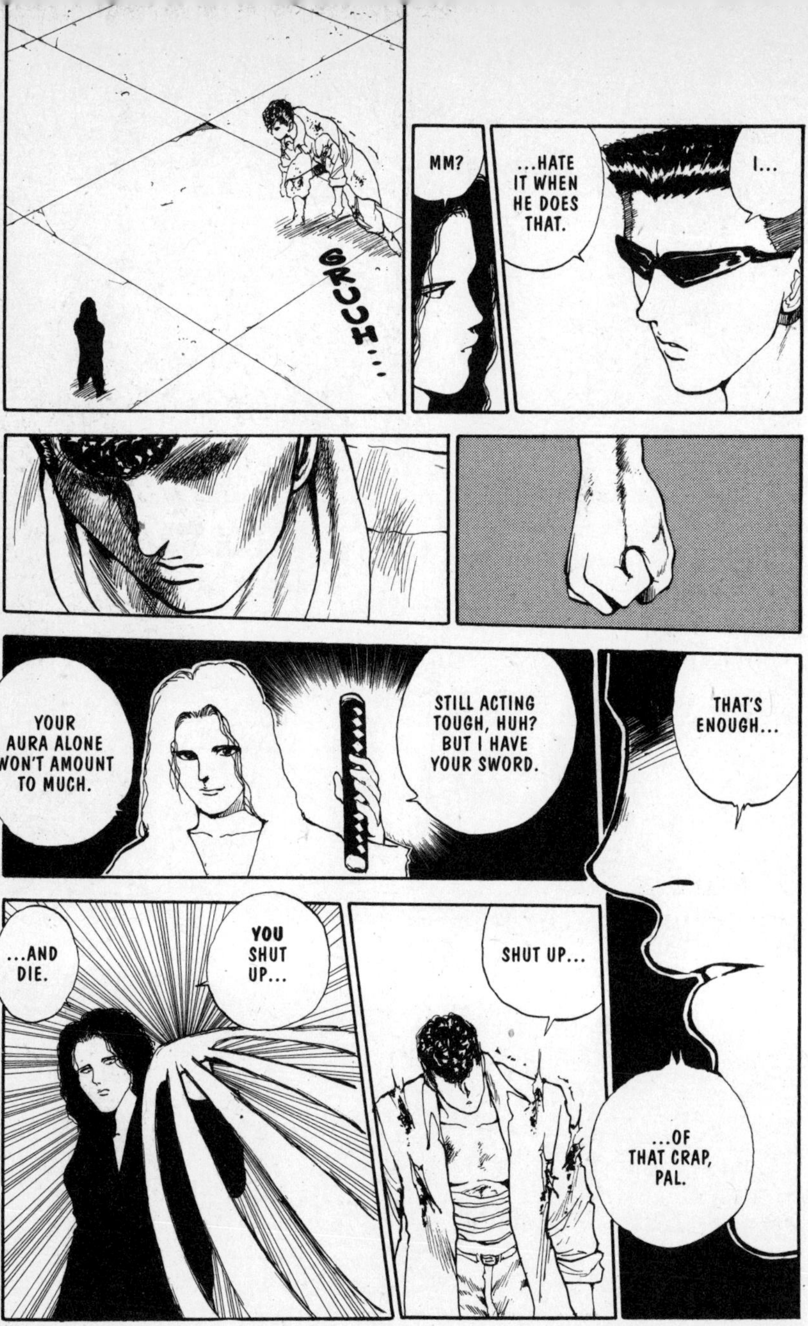
I...
...HATE IT WHEN HE DOES THAT.
MM?
GRUUH...
THAT'S ENOUGH...
STILL ACTING TOUGH, HUH? BUT I HAVE YOUR SWORD.
YOUR AURA ALONE WON'T AMOUNT TO MUCH.
...OF THAT CRAP, PAL.
SHUT UP...
YOU SHUT UP...
...AND DIE.

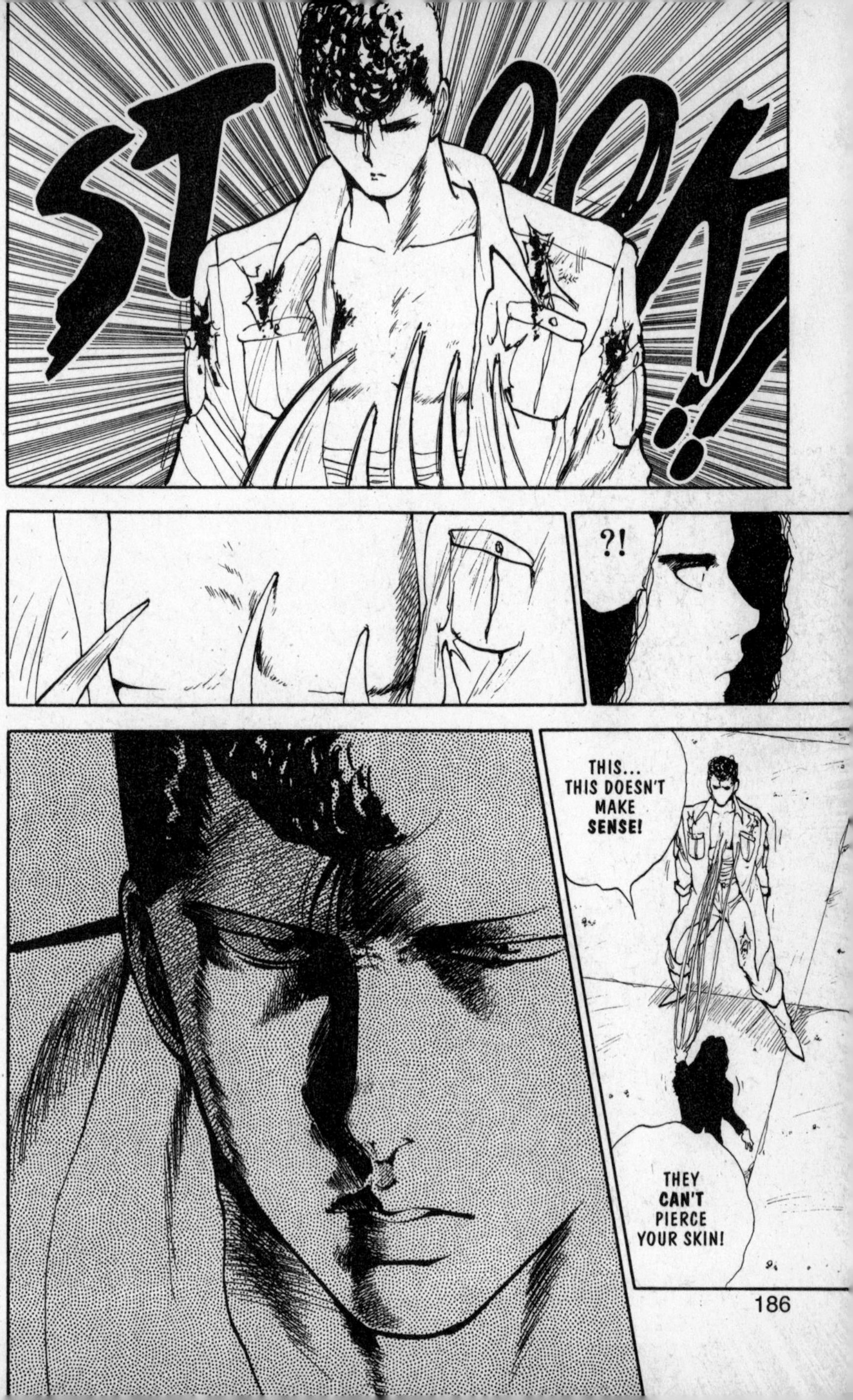
STOOOF!!
?!
THIS... THIS DOESN'T MAKE **SENSE!**
THEY **CAN'T** PIERCE YOUR SKIN!

READ THIS WAY

COMING NEXT VOLUME...

The fight you've been waiting for has finally arrived and it's totally intense! With the death of Genkai, Urameshi's got a lot of fuel to feed his angry fighting fire! However, the younger Toguro has been purposely stoking his flames trying to see how hot they can get! Who will prevail in this insane showdown?

Coming May 2007

Read it first in *SHONEN JUMP* magazine!

LAST SAIYAN STANDING!
DRAGON BALL Z™
On sale now!
DRAGON BALL Z
THANK YOU! GOOD BYE!!
SHONEN JUMP MANGA
Story & Art by Akira Toriyama
volume 26
DRAGON BALL Z
SHONEN JUMP GRAPHIC NOVEL
Story & Art by Akira Toriyama
volume 1
On sale at:
WWW.SHONENJUMP.COM
Also available at your local bookstore and comic store.
viz media
SHONEN JUMP MANGA
DRAGON BALL © 1984 by BIRD STUDIO/SHUEISHA Inc.

SUBSCRIBE TODAY & BECOME A MEMBER OF THE SHONEN JUMP SUBSCRIBER CLUB...
You'll get:
*Access to Exclusive Online Content!
*50% Savings Off the Newsstand Price!
*Exclusive Premiums!
All this available ONLY to Subscribers!
SHONEN JUMP
THE WORLD'S MOST POPULAR MANGA
FILL OUT THE SUBSCRIPTION CARD ON THE OTHER SIDE, OR SUBSCRIBE ONLINE AT:
www.shonenjump.com